Praise for Antanas S

"... *Some Unfinished Business* is a moving, page-turning examination of loyalty, betrayal, retribution and ultimately, love, written by an acclaimed author at the height of his powers."
—*Gary Barwin, author of* Yiddish for Pirates

"*The Barefoot Bingo Caller* is evocative, unfailingly honest, and dead-on funny! A masterful piece of writing."
—*Miriam Toews, author of* Women Talking

On *Underground*: "... an example of the elegant thinking that characterizes this rare and compelling chronicle."
—*Donna Bailey Nurse in* The Globe and Mail

On *Provisionally Yours*: "... an urbane thriller."
—*Publishers Weekly*

On *Woman in Bronze*: "... written in deceptively easy prose ... superbly told." —*Michael Redhill in* The Globe and Mail

On *Buying on Time*: "Antanas Sileika has made a significant contribution to the body of immigrant literature."
—*Philip Marchand in the* Toronto Star

On *Dinner at the End of the World*: "The art is in the telling, and these stories are wonderfully told."
—*Wayne Grady in the* Toronto Star

"Antanas Sileika is one of the quiet stars of CanLit, creating memorable, complex, and enthralling stories in his five novels and his memoir." —*Open Book interview*

THE
DEATH
OF
TONY

Also by Antanas Sileika

Some Unfinished Business
Provisionally Yours
The Barefoot Bingo Caller
Underground
Woman in Bronze
Buying on Time
Dinner at the End of the World

THE DEATH OF
ON TONY
BELONGING IN TWO WORLDS

antanas sileika

STONEHEWER
BOOKS

ISBN: 978-1-7389933-4-5
eBook ISBN: 978-1-7389933-5-2

1 2 3 4 5 6 7 8 9 10

Anne Applebaum excerpt originally published as "The Worst of the Madness" in *The New York Review of Books*, November 11 2010. Copyright © 2010, Anne Applebaum.

Ray Bradbury's *The Martian Chronicles* © 1950, renewed 1978, courtesy of Ray Bradbury Literary Works, LLC.

Cataloguing Data available from Library and Archives Canada.

Author photograph by Liudas Masys
Set in Coranto and Catalpa by Ned Seager

Printed and bound in Canada by Friesens

Stonehewer Books | Victoria, BC
stonehewerbooks.com

Stonehewer Books is located on the traditional territory of the Lkwungen people on what is now called Vancouver Island. We acknowledge and are grateful for the unique contributions to our common well-being made by the Indigenous peoples of this land.

J'ai deux amours

A song made popular by Josephine Baker in 1930

for

Andy and Joe
a.k.a
Audris and Juozas

Contents

Two Worlds in Suspension   1

Weston   11

Micks and Brits   19

Lithuanian Christmas in Canada   27

The Endless (Lithuanian) Summer (Camp)   34

Lithuanian School, High School, and Girls   42

The Death of Tony   56

Paris   77

Two Lithuanian Jews in London   93

Goodbye to All That   100

The Lithuanian Language Strikes Back   110

The Personal Becomes Political   116

Turning Away, Turning Back   132

Professor Sileika in the Literary Trenches   147

New Roots   158

Reflections Toward a Hill of Cherry Trees   169

A Little History   176

The Hometown is Always There for You   183

As for Me and My Place   191

Remembering and Forgetting   198

Then and Now   212

The Afterlife of the Strato Chief   216

A Moving Target   220

one

Two Worlds in Suspension

IN 1958, WHEN I WAS FIVE, MY FATHER BOUGHT OUR first new car in Canada, a forest-green Strato Chief with plenty of chrome trim, including a spray of stars along each of the rear sections.

We were shooting into the future.

The Strato Chief was a leap ahead of the used low panel van my father had been driving to construction jobs. As required by law, my mother had painted my father's name and trade, "carpenter," across the side just behind the single passenger door. Never entirely patient in handwriting, she'd let some of the paint drip here and there, so the lettering's imperfection emphasized the authenticity of our limited means. My mother didn't care. She claimed sloppy handwriting was the sign of educated people who needed to write fast to keep up with their university lectures. Why should she care about labels anyway?

That old van had no seats in the back; we three boys sat on a loose legless couch at a time when nobody took seatbelts seriously. What could go wrong? There were no side windows there either, so we always looked only forward (or back if we craned our necks).

The Strato Chief was just one piece of our good fortune. A few years earlier, my mother had lucked into a job as a food chemist for the federal government, employers whose bureaucracy was so slow it took almost two years to send along the back pay from a raise. When it arrived, it came as a lump sum. A few hundred dollars! Enough to buy an empty lot north of Toronto at Wasaga Beach on Georgian Bay, a couple of hours away, and to fund the materials to build the shell of a cottage. As long as we did the work ourselves.

By 1961, my parents' family was living according to the postwar playbook we see in movies and old television shows. Suburban house, new car, and three boys in t-shirts and jeans in the back seat. At eighteen, brother Andy was the oldest, a lean hockey player, and Joe at fourteen was already knocking baseballs out of the school playground. At age eight, I sat between them, my legs on the hump in the floor. I was called Tony in those days and would be for another dozen years. One Tony and so many others like him in the landscape of those suburban days.

Andy, Joe, and Tony. Canadian boys in the glow of postwar prosperity.

Even our father, with his perpetually smoking pipe, could have been a version of the television figure Father Knows Best, if seen from afar. But from closer up, one or another of his gold teeth glinted when he smiled, and there was nothing measured or calm whenever he got exasperated or when he shared his opinions, of which he had many.

"Poor people have only themselves to blame if they go hungry."

"Dad, come on. Lots of unfortunate people go hungry."

"Have they never heard of rabbits? They breed faster than you can eat them."

Nobody we knew ate rabbits and they didn't sell them in the supermarkets. But how was it possible to answer his remark? We didn't know anything about rabbits.

Another of my father's firmly held opinions was that a radio in a car was a waste of money, arguably a dangerous distraction from the serious business of driving. But talk was permitted, even encouraged, and we came from a family of talkers, when not sulking.

The frequent weekend trips to build a cottage gave our parents the opportunity to remind us that although we lived in a country as glorious as ancient Rome, minus the fancy architecture and flowing gowns, this Canadian place was as nothing compared to their home in Lithuania. That was the Troy they had fled, with the scent of fire and death behind them.

They would never have thought in those terms because they didn't have any classics in their education. That's me, only one year of Latin in high school and I'm always reaching for allusions. They would find ridiculous any comparison between small-town Ontario and Rome, provincial Lithuania and Troy. They were striving toward prosperity, and I eventually became a striver too, an immigrant boy with linguistic pretensions.

The front seat told stories about the past. The back seat was too young to have stories yet. We just had fantasies about the future.

IN EARLY JULY OF 1944, my mother is in the garden of their house in Alytus, the provincial capital, playing with her infant son Audris, the future Andy, who can toddle along while she holds one of his hands. The linden trees are full of blossoms and the roses have just passed their first bloom.

A scholarship graduate in chemistry and math, she had wanted to go into medicine but hated Latin. Instead, she became a multidisciplinary educator. She is a busy mother and also director of the Alytus teachers' college, a high post for someone only twenty-seven years old, and she's tired because there seem to have been a lot of parties recently, as though the war could be jollied away one evening at a time if one drank, ate, and joked enough. She never paid much attention to politics, even during the worst of the hostilities.

My mother turns to the maid, who has come to ask what she wants for dinner. My mother remarks that the windows on the second floor of their house are very dirty.

The maid says the Red Army will be in Alytus within a week. My mother should worry about other things.

She is shocked. She waits for my father to come home from work as a criminal police officer in the town. He then tells her he already has a horse and wagon, money, and cured meats, as well as topographical maps so they can avoid the major roads on their trip west through Nazi Germany. There is no other way out.

Is it really necessary to go? Yes. His brother, Antanas, has called to say they must flee. Antanas spent a year under interrogation and lost his teeth through beatings during the first Soviet occupation four years earlier. Now the Soviets are coming back. Ironically, another brother, Aleksandras, the eldest, a farmer, is the one with the least bourgeois nationalist profile, but he is the one who will stay behind in his naïveté and be shipped out to die in the gulag for his belief in his innocence.

She asks what she can do.

My father tells her to dry as much bread as she can. Dried bread is one of those staples that Eastern Europeans have used to survive famine in times of war. Buckwheat is another, but who knows if there will be time to cook as they flee.

IN THE BACK SEAT of the Strato Chief, I didn't even know what buckwheat was, but the mention of food made me hungry. My mother had roasted a chicken with potatoes and carrots the night before, and that morning put the black tin roasting pan on the car floor. To save time on our arrival, she would just heat it up. The knowledge of this nearby chicken made me impatient with the injustice of the situation — food close by yet forbidden to us by the imperious rules of our parents.

THEY LEAVE ALYTUS IN A COVERED WAGON of the kind I saw on TV Westerns, pulled by a local breed of small horse not much bigger than a pony. My mother's teenage sister, a dark-haired beauty long known as "Schwartze Jane," rides along with them. My father owns a motorcycle, but gasoline is hard to come by, so he affixes it to the back of the wagon and they tow it along for a while until it becomes awkward. One night, my father digs a pit, greases up the motorcycle, and buries it so he can get it back when they return, as they expect to do not long in the future.

THE STORY OF THIS BURIED MOTORCYCLE distracted me from my hunger, and I imagined returning for it one day when I grew up. From his place before the steering wheel at the front of the Strato Chief, my father removed his pipe from between his teeth, laughed, and said it might still be there.

THE GERMANS ARE IN RETREAT and their impositions on refugees are unpredictable. One sergeant wants to take my beautiful aunt for a labour battalion, and who knows what else, but my father has forged documents from the German administration saying he is on an important mission.

How could this story of his be plausible to German authority? A baby and a couple of women along on some kind of important mission? But Germans respect documents, if not much else. My aunt is not taken away.

They flee for a few days and wait, overnighting in the yards of local parish priests until the sound of the front gets closer. The German border at Prussia is closed, and then it melts and a flood of refugees bursts out, heading west. My father is careful to stay on small country roads. Because of the baby, my parents seem unthreatening to local farmers, and they are usually allowed to stay in the barns. Once, the infant and mother are permitted to stay inside the house. It is a very fine house, a big place with heavy furniture and inhabited by an elegant and melancholy older couple.

The man sees my mother looking at a chair in the dining room where the table has been pulled aside. On the floor around the chair lies human hair.

"My son's hair," says the man. "He was home on leave and his mother was cutting his hair when the Gestapo came for him."

My mother doesn't know what to say.

"He opposed the war," says the man. His wife says nothing at all. My mother wonders how long ago all of this happened but is glad to spend the night in a bed and accepts the offer of milk for the child.

IN THE BACK OF THE CAR, I had no idea who Prussians were. Later, I'd find out they were considered guilty for Germany's militarism. They had to pay for their crimes. So all the Prussians were driven out of their part of the country or killed. Only orphans, called "wolf children," were left to wander about and survive as best they could.

AT TIMES, IT SEEMS AS IF the front has frozen. My father offers help on farms where there are no farmhands or even adolescents any longer. The men, old and young, have been taken by the German army. But my father never helps out for long because the sounds of war approach and the family must flee again. Once, they cut their departure a little too close. They are in a stream of refugees desperate not to be overtaken by the Soviets. Maybe the tide will turn again, but if it doesn't, far, far better to end up under the Americans, the British, or the French.

My mother learns to distinguish the engines of Soviet planes from those of others. The Soviets fire on the refugee columns, but others do not. At the sound of a Soviet engine, she leaps from the wagon for a ditch, and my father has to take the baby in his arms and join my mother and her sister. From his place in the ditch, my father comes to admire their small horse, which stands calmly as bullets fly around it upon the roadway.

Finally it is evening and they have been on the road for a long time. The horse is tired and they have been fired upon more than once during the day and they would like to rest, but a soldier tells them a bridge at a nearby river is going to be blown up to slow the Soviet advance. They must get across the bridge or they will be trapped on the Soviet side.

Many people are waiting to cross and the Germans have their orders and might blow the bridge at any moment. But by night they finally make it across and when they reach the other side and pull into a field to rest, my father unhitches the horse and it lies down on its side.

"Who wants an apple?"

My mother offered them to the boys in the back seat because the line of stalled traffic seemed to lead all the way to the horizon and the car was stifling due to my father's fear of drafts.

I didn't want an apple. I wanted the chicken in the roasting pan.

"Do you know how tired a horse has to be to lie down on its side?" my mother asked.

We didn't know anything about horses aside from what we had seen on television. Horses belonged to another era, to cowboys and Indians.

So we munched away in the back seat and Andy rolled down the window (the back windows only went halfway down) and threw the core into the ditch.

The story had been OK. It had helped to fill the boring hours in the car, but it was not as compelling as the friends we were going to see at the beach, the basketball games my brother would play, or the swing I'd sit upon with my girlfriend, Gracie, who had promised to marry me when we grew up.

And the story was not something I'd think about very often in the years in the suburb where we lived. My friends meant everything to me, and their parents and mine were bit players, stock characters on the fringes of our main stage.

There were a lot of stories beneath the surface of our suburb, but we kids weren't all that interested. Those stories came from the past. We were interested in the future.

two
Weston

DISPLACED PERSONS (DP) CAMPS DOTTED WESTERN EU-
rope after the war, and my parents ended up in one in Oldenburg, in West Germany, in 1945. There they waited for
the allies to push back the Soviets, but that didn't happen.

At first, the allies wanted Eastern Europeans to go
home after the war. Some in the British occupation zone
of Germany, primarily Cossacks, were forced back to
the Soviet Union and found themselves in the gulag or
worse. Some others forced to return to Yugoslavia were
shot on arrival.

The allies decided they needed to do something with
these refugees and thought about it for a few years. The
DP camps were a holding zone waiting for a decision,
and then Belgium finally discovered it was short of mine
workers. Other countries began to open their doors too,
and in 1948, single men and women and sponsored
families were permitted to emigrate to Canada.

In Oldenburg, my parents had had another baby before finding a long-lost cousin in Ontario's Fort William
to sponsor their emigration to Canada. In the beginning,

my mother was a bunkhouse cook on a big farm and my father was a night watchman, keeping the barn's woodstoves going so the cows did not freeze. Seeing no future there, they moved first to Toronto and then to nearby Weston.

IT WAS STILL A SMALL TOWN in the 1950s and '60s, but the city of Toronto was encroaching on Weston and the town in its turn was expanding into the farm fields around it, fields that had been bought but not yet developed. Within these unplanted fields stood a few abandoned farm houses with broken windows, and on the ground lay ponds slick with slime; the untended vegetation was beginning to include Queen Anne's lace, milkweed, and poplar saplings.

In this suburb-to-be lived a scattering of working-class and middle-class families, deposited there by the postwar boom. In North America, the lucky ones remember this time fondly as one of wealth and growth, and in the USA, slow enlightenment about civil rights. But it had its vestigial postwar horrors. Later I would find out my friend of Japanese heritage, Mike, had parents who were interned as aliens during the war and lost all of their property. My friend Allen's father had been a Canadian soldier in Hong Kong when it fell to the invading Japanese army, and he spent the war in a prisoner of war camp where he lost most of his sight due to malnutrition.

There must have been a Lithuanian real estate salesman who lured my father out to Weston, because he wasn't the only one of his kind there. A couple dozen Lithuanian immigrant families peppered the new subdivisions growing up around the town.

My father and his friends dug out the basement by hand, and the year before I was born, my parents and brothers lived illegally underground. They didn't have the money to build the ground floor yet, so they paid off one town building inspector and bamboozled another by pretending to be ignorant immigrants who didn't speak the language. To the horror of the more "advanced" Canadian neighbours living across the way, they also had an outhouse, with newspaper squares carefully cut out and stacked beside the seat. My father said only a fool would buy paper that was destined for a short trip from your bum to the pit below.

One day, my mother went into the hospital and my father fried a mountain of hamburgers and put them in the fridge. My father and brothers ate hamburgers, hot or cold, at every meal until my mother brought me home as the new baby in 1953.

Now there were five of us. My mother fell into depression right after I was born, stuck as she was in a basement in what seemed like a remote town, with a husband who kept getting laid off factory work. My father later told me he counted milk bottles after he got home from work each day to make sure she hadn't forgotten to feed me in her despair.

The house was finally finished, a so-called "one-and-a-half." My parents rented two rooms and a miniscule kitchen upstairs to a family of four, but they had to share their single bathroom with those of us from downstairs. We five and my aunt lived below, at a time when one bathroom among ten people did not seem unusual. Before I went to kindergarten, the mother upstairs looked after me. This arrangement permitted my mother to rally and find work in a factory packing cookies. My father gave up factory work to become a construction carpenter.

This whole story was mostly prehistory to me. By the time I grew old enough to have memories, my mother had found a job as a chemist and my father worked the whole construction season long, breaking only in winter.

The hardest days were past.

RESIDENTIAL OLD WESTON was a fine town with tall trees and century homes, but we were in a suburb on its shoulder. 22 Langside Avenue stood on the crest of a low hill, with another nineteen houses on both sides down the block. This stretch made the core of my childhood world. Beside our house lay a double lot of wasteland, with a dugout "fort" the size of a large dining room table where my middle brother and his friends performed the ritual of burning their notebooks at the end of the elementary school year.

After a few years, a Baptist church would grow up on the lot, another kind of imaginary fort we crawled over as it was being built. Then it became a building we chased one another around while playing war games. My mother called me in once when she found me using an inferior plastic water pistol as my weapon. She gave me two dollars to go to Kresge's on Weston's main street and buy myself a decent toy rifle.

Our sloping street was fine for throwing baseballs or footballs, but too unfavourable for the downhill team if we played road hockey, so we moved down to where my friend David's family had the first paved driveway, one that lay flat. Our gang had six boys around the same age, and a few younger and older sisters and brothers as auxiliaries. We were territorial, and sometimes we'd go to war with kids our age who lived on other streets. We'd throw clods of dirt that almost never hit their mark and make threatening gestures with sticks, though we never came to actual blows.

Above these streets all summer long there lingered the smell of cut grass, the scent of suburbs, the perfume of our days.

As A KID I was always hungry, and the uniformity of suburban life was broken into a mosaic when it came to food.

While I was playing in one backyard, David's "Canadian" mother gave me Wonder Bread slices, deliciously soft. I could bite off the crusts, crush the white into a tight knob in my fist, and then suck on it in my mouth for some time, prolonging the taste. If Lithuanian mothers did offer bread, it was heavy rye spread thickly with blackcurrant jam, the flavours of Eastern Europe. I loved hot dogs, ideally on hot dog buns because my father refused to buy them, insisting they were a marketing ploy. Regular bread could be wrapped around a hot dog just as well.

Canadian backyards were mostly lawns with flowers at the borders. In season, Lithuanian yards had blackcurrants, redcurrants, plums, pears, rhubarb, and modest cucumbers mysteriously hard to find in the low scratchy jungle of their growth.

WESTON HAD BEEN SETTLED since 1881. The heyday of its main street is the kind that has been mimicked again and again in ironic film sets like *American Graffitti* or *Back to the Future* or even Dolly Parton's fantasy Christmas special about some kind of ideal small town.

We didn't live in geography tinged with irony — we just lived: Inch's drugstore, with the soda fountain; the pool hall for local toughs; women's dress shops, in which my aunt made me wait interminably in my hot winter coat as she negotiated the purchase of another new dress, although she hadn't paid for the two dresses before that. It would eventually take a new husband to walk the shops to clear her debts after they got married.

The Carnegie Library was a consolation to a kid no good at sports. It was a kind of private place, where you could explore who you might become, depending on what you chose to read from among the books on the shelves. I found solace in the children's room below until I was thirteen and was finally allowed upstairs. Having no guide to tell me what to read, I started with a biography of Rasputin but saw no opportunity to become him. Instead I found others, among them Dylan Thomas, first in print and later on vinyl records.

Finally, there was Squibb's Stationers, today's only survivor of Old Weston, the place where in high school I made a little pocket money by sweeping the floors and washing the windows and working with many genial middle-aged women who came in for a few hours each week. Old Mr. Squibb, the son of the founder, worked in a small office in the back but was called upon rarely because of his bad heart. The women watched over him and tutted as he fingered a too-long cigarette butt someone had left behind in the ashtray. He sighed over his lost youth and the freedom to smoke. The cellar was my realm, where I was sent to cut bristol board with the guillotine or to count the miniature notepads to be sure we had enough to restock the shelves above.

OUR SUBURB HAD SMALL HOUSES on big lots, a variety of them, some built by the people who lived in them and some built by small developers who struck it rich or went broke, according to the moment in history. They were postwar bungalows, with two or three bedrooms and the back door not on the back but on the side. Later, wider houses went up, with attached garages and roofs that sloped smartly to one side, like berets set on the heads of travel poster Frenchmen.

AND THEN THERE WERE the empty fields beyond the top of our street, where later the expressways and more suburbs would be built, but where in my childhood lay a whole world of weed-choked fields and forgotten apple trees. Black Creek was a stream I could jump over, and I rambled through the nearby wasteland. So did hobos, whose cold fire pits and empty tins of beans we would sometimes find, as well as mickeys of Five Star whiskey drained to the last drop, the caps long gone as if they were cast off the moment the men opened the bottles.

I lacked nothing in these places; everything I needed was there. I could be a town boy drinking Cokes in Weston, a suburban boy riding my bicycle in the subdivision, or a country boy picking my way along the fallen fence posts in the abandoned farm fields with a stalk of grass between my teeth.

What else could anyone want?

three
Micks and Brits

SOME KIDS WENT UP THE STREET TO THE PUBLIC SCHOOL
kindergarten, but I was taken on the slightly longer walk
down the street to the Catholic one in the convent. My
father suspected you might *really* burn in hell for missing
Mass on Sunday, so it was best to fill as much of your life
with Catholicism as possible just to be on the safe side,
just to have a little extra credibility when you met your
maker.

On the first day in the convent kindergarten — an
old red-brick house with three chimneys, practically a
mansion, on a wooded street in Old Weston — I proudly
wore a bright blue blazer. Even though I'd been born
in Canada, a blazer marked our family as Europeans,
new immigrants, still functioning according to foreign
norms. I had no knee socks, so the uniform was not
completely old-fashioned, but I didn't look like a kid
about to play on the street. More like the child of a
mother trying to prove something.

I was happy among the puzzles and thick pencils and
paper the nuns laid out for us after we returned from

daily prayers in the chapel. In all things I wanted to emulate my older brothers, and since they were in school, I wanted to be in school too. Other boys stood for days crying at the window for their mothers, but I didn't understand them. To me it seemed as silly as crying in an amusement park, albeit one with very firm rules.

The black-clad nuns were all called "Mother" and there seemed to be a lot of them, young and old. They did not feel *exactly* like mothers, but they felt comfortable enough to me, more like an army of aunts who bustled about in various adult ways when not teaching us songs or prayers. We played outside on the vast lawn and drank cocoa on the massive veranda where the lemon tarts my mother had packed for me as a snack were envied by the other kids and I could buy "best friend" status by offering small bites. My only horror was the cocoa itself, which must have been boiled because it developed a skin on the surface that clung to the lips of the children, hanging down over their chins like ugly tongues.

My middle brother, Joe, was supposed to walk me home as he passed by from elementary school, but one day he was late. Exasperated, I walked home by myself, and it never occurred to one of my "mothers" to prevent me from doing so. When my parents found out I knew the way, they decided that at five I was old enough to take care of myself, and I was allowed to come home each day on my own. The boarders upstairs could let me in, but they soon moved out and I was given my own key. If ever I forgot it, I would crawl inside through the milk box at the back of our house.

IN GRADE ONE, I walked to the Catholic school with my best friend John and his older sister, who lived down the street. His name was Gintautas at home, but just as I was Tony to him, he was John to me and our friends, unless I was speaking to his parents, who were Lithuanian too.

In St. John the Evangelist Elementary School, we learned first to be proper Catholics and second to be loyal subjects of the British Commonwealth. Those fealties were most important. Arithmetic, English, and physical education came third, fourth, and fifth, although English might be advanced on the list of priorities if you were a child who had just immigrated with your parents. Most immigrants at the time were Italians. Then, you sat at the back of the class until you picked up enough language to be moved forward.

We carried statues of the virgin around the school halls on certain feast days and went to Mass every first Friday of the month in the church next door. Sometimes, if I was early to school, I'd duck into morning Mass to be among the eight or nine adults and a couple of kids who showed up there. I dreamed of being an altar boy but was hopeless in learning the Latin prayers. Altar boys had an annual picnic in the middle of the school day, and they received tips at christenings, funerals, and baptisms.

There were grades of altar boys, like there were grades in Scouts. It seemed such a privilege that the older altar boys be permitted to kneel in shifts day and night in the church from Holy Thursday to Easter Sunday, in perpetual adoration of the host until the purple Lenten sacks came off the statues.

The church was staffed with an old and severe senior priest and a young, energetic one whom all the kids loved. We had to line up for confession once a month, and the line before the young priest's confessional was long. Only the pious or courageous chose the old priest, and when his line diminished, he would open his door and beckon to some of us to come to him. We were horrified not only because he was so serious, but because once he had chosen us, we had lost our anonymity, which was supposed to be our right as we confessed our childish "sins."

The Lithuanian Catholic church was a half hour drive away, so we usually used the local church instead. I sang briefly in the choir until the choirmaster realized my voice was ruining his reputation. During Mass itself, my clever brother Joe learned to tap the bottom of the offerings basket so the change jingled inside and made it sound as if he had put a coin in to join the others instead of palming it in his hand.

I didn't think much about the church, which was always there, unless it was to recognize even when I was very small that short candles meant Low Mass — maybe forty minutes long — and tall candles meant High Mass, well over an hour of suffering for an easily bored kid. We had the Baptist church next door to our house, and although we might play on the street with one or another of the Baptist kids, we knew the inside of that church was forbidden territory. The women who came out of that church seemed to have finer hats than the Catholic women, and sometimes they even wore gloves if it was Easter.

We were led into church from the school in Grades Seven and Eight. My friend Vaughan and I would roll dice on the pew between us to gamble away our hockey cards. Vaughan was a brash, dark-haired whirlwind who I admired unless he turned on me, which happened from time to time. Once I was sitting below him on a small hill and he decided I was being insufficiently subservient to him, so he rose and charged down on me. I wasn't much of a fighter, but I needed to rise fast and I reached to grab hold of him to lift myself up. Without intending to, I grabbed between his legs, so as I pulled to raise myself up, he went down with a howl, and that was the end of the fight.

I respected Vaughan because he was *English*. His parents both spoke with traces of an English accent and his father drove a Bentley and I admired them for these things. But their Englishness might have been hybrid, had I thought about it, because how many English were Catholics? Were they originally Irish micks? I didn't know the word then, but later, one of my brothers told me if someone called me a mick to punch him in the nose.

I admired all things British. I read British boys' adventure stories and Kipling, Conan Doyle, and Wells. I aspired to a stiff upper lip and insensitivity to any claims against not only the Commonwealth but also the Empire that had come before it. I loved the Commonwealth and felt proud to be a part of it.

In school the world map hung open at all times and the Commonwealth countries, from India to Hong Kong to Australia and Canada, were coloured pink to show their fealty to the queen. She had come to her position, by happy circumstance, the year I was born, and so she felt like a kind of British godmother.

DEEP UNDER THIS IMPERIAL SPELL, I came to think of myself as not only British, but English, managing to maintain this belief even in the face of never speaking English with my parents. Like Walt Whitman, I felt no contradiction — I contained multitudes. But the fantasy could only be maintained so long.

When Vaughan's grandmother came to visit, I sat with the family as she distributed gifts to her grandchildren.

Although obviously there would be no gift for me, I felt as if I, too, was part of this family circle, confirmed in its Englishness by the much stronger accent of Vaughan's grandmother.

Then she turned to look at me kindly and said, "What a beautiful boy this is. Such a shame that he's a foreigner."

So MANY WORDS have been spoken to me in my life, so many words forgotten, yet these ones remain very clear. Was I hurt? Oh yes! But her words were useful to me in the long run. She woke me up — she tore away my fantasy. It seemed I could not be English. Over the years, I learned I would need to be something else.

But if my Englishness was erased, I didn't feel as if the pink parts of the map had been taken from me. I still harboured a love for them, although my love was evolving from empire and commonwealth to language alone.

When I was older, a smoking teenager, on hot summer's days I would go down to the cool basement of my parents' house with a quart of chocolate milk and a package of cigarettes and pass the time down there listening to Dylan Thomas reading his poetry or radio plays, in particular *Under Milk Wood* and *A Child's Christmas in Wales*. I adored the melody of his voice, which now seems too rich, too flowery, too posh, but which then spoke deeply to me. Other English texts did the same: the King James Bible, in particular the psalms, and some of Shakespeare, especially the Saint Crispin's Day speech, which even now, well into my old age, I'm afraid to listen to in public in case my lips start to tremble and worse follows.

So Kipling and the Queen, the Empire and the Commonwealth were not for this foreigner boy, but I came out with a prize nonetheless. I kept the gift of the English language.

four
Lithuanian Christmas in Canada (With a Nod to Dylan Thomas)

YEARS AND YEARS AGO, WHEN THERE WERE STILL PACKS of half-wild dogs allowed to wander on the streets and fields of Weston, Christmases felt like they would never change. And then they did change. Again and again.

We had twin Christmases. One for our Canadian side and another for our Lithuanian side.

There was "English Christmas," as we called it, celebrated on Christmas Day. We recognized all things Canadian at the time as more or less "English," meaning "normal," the more Dickensian the better. We were barely aware of Quebec and what they did there, to say nothing of our ignorance of Indigenous culture.

We adopted the Canadian Christmas Day celebration because why should you only have one party when you can have two? *Kūčios*, our Lithuanian Christmas Eve celebration, was intended as holy, even solemn. Kūčios wasn't ever intended as *merry*, let alone *jolly*, but it evolved to be so in our house.

The first Canadian Kūčios took place before I was born,

27

as described by my oldest brother. That was in the early 1950s when my father and mother were new immigrants living in a partially completed house on the edge of Weston with my two older brothers. Kūčios meant kneeling for prayers on Christmas Eve and then eating some herring before going to bed. This was the austere picture of the struggling immigrants, far from extended family yet clinging to Lithuanian tradition in a modest way.

It didn't stay that way long.

The Kūčios I remember, as the youngest member of the family, came about a decade later. For those of us living at 22 Langside Avenue, Kūčios had become something like a birthday party, a big booze-up with religious overtones. Lithuanian Kūčios collided with English Christmas, and English Christmas was like a blend of Charles Dickens and the American Dream. Initially, besides my immediate family, there were only my childless aunt and her husband, and we would wait for this couple to arrive at our house after work on Christmas Eve.

This was in the period of the early 1960s, the high point of North American postwar prosperity, more than a decade after my parents had come to Canada and found good jobs that paid well. Our suburban street was filled with houses extravagantly covered with Christmas lights, and a few years later, we would sometimes drive out in one of the two cars we owned during the Christmas season to look at the Christmas lights of the richer neighbourhoods or at shop windows downtown. When I reflect about the two cars, I am amazed. My mother never learned to drive, but we eventually bought a second car so my older brothers could give her a ride in case my father was busy. Nobody thought this was extravagant.

My mother would take time off work and laboured for days at home leading up to the double holiday. She would barely sleep the night before Kūčios, cooking Lithuanian dishes such as herring with onions and tomato for my father and Canadian dishes for her sons: fried mushrooms, smoked haddock in cream sauce over boiled potatoes, deep-fried smelts served crispy or submerged in mild vinaigrette. I had to peel shrimp for my mother but we mostly tried to avoid her because she was frenzied and looking for us to help her. All the while she had to keep an eye on my father, who would have liked to start drinking well before noon and sometimes did if she didn't watch him carefully.

When my sequined aunt and her slicked-back husband arrived, we'd go to the table for a quiet moment of sharing the sheets of traditional Christmas unleavened bread (*plotkelės*) with one another. Then everyone would eat two or three days' worth of cooking in about twenty minutes. Tradition said we should have twelve meat-free dishes, the number of apostles, but we often had fourteen or fifteen because who knew, maybe there were more apostles who hadn't been able to make it on time for the Last Supper? Men drank shots of vodka and sipped on chaser cocktails of rye and ginger all night. Women drank shots too, but they tended to sip them and not take quite as many. Three of the adults smoked, so the room was full of alcohol fumes, pipe and cigarette smoke, and the smell of fried fish.

Our table was always roaring with volume that exceeded what you would expect from our modest numbers. Everyone in our family was a storyteller but not many were listeners, and everyone spoke loudly, usually at the same time. In later years we opened our gifts that evening, but in earlier years we saved them for Christmas Day in order to be like the Canadians, who were like the English. Thus, Christmas Eve was our Lithuanian evening, and Christmas Day was our Canadian day.

But Kūčios was far from over yet. Drinking, eating, shouting, and smoking all went on for hours until it was time to go to Midnight Mass at the Lithuanian parish. When we arrived at church, my parents and aunt and uncle went up to get seats and listen to the choir before Mass, but teenagers and young people hung around the doors to talk to one another.

Young people hoped that there was as little room in the pews as possible, so we wouldn't have to sit with our parents and could stand around the back doors of the church in the vestibule, like Catholic gangsters who were too tough to sit at Mass but too Catholic to skip it.

If we did stand in the back, we could practically see the haze of alcohol over the parishioners, and we'd laugh quietly at the odd drunk who fell asleep. And if we were at the back, our mothers watched carefully to make sure we showed up at the communion rail and were not just gabbing with friends in the church basement below. My suspicious father might later ask what we thought of the priest's homily, and we were expected to report in detail.

Then it was quick goodbyes to friends and home before about two a.m. when my mother would take out the ham and start serving shots to my uncle, who liked to stay up late. My father, on the other hand, went to bed and liked to get up early. Therefore my mother got almost no sleep at all.

The next morning was English Christmas. First, my father and uncle had a couple of shots to take the hair of the dog. Then there was a little free time as my mother prepared a turkey to be eaten early in the afternoon. As an enthusiast of all things British, I made the impossibly heavy plum pudding, which I covered with brandy and lit up and brought burning to the table, although everyone was so full that hardly anybody ate it. This in yet another tobacco haze and after more shots and more cocktails.

In this respect, English Christmas and Lithuanian Kūčios were similar — namely, alcoholic and gluttonous. How did we manage in those days to consume the evening Kūčios dishes, the middle of the night ham, and then the afternoon turkey?

My aunt and her husband were gone by the middle of Christmas Day, but my father managed a few more shots before collapsing into bed by the middle of the afternoon. He would barely get up any more that day unless it was to go to the bathroom or have another drink.

My exhausted mother might take a nap too, but she would be up by early evening in order to enjoy a little quiet time with her sons. But her sons were youths who wanted to go out with their friends, so we would sulk until she finally relented and let us go, and we left her all alone with an empty house except for a snoring husband who would be hungover badly the next day with no cure at hand because she had hidden whatever alcohol remained in the house.

TWO DECADES LATER, Kūčios changed again when I married. By then one of my brothers had married too, and in the end there were close to twenty of us in our holiday celebrations.

OUR PARENTS' GENERATION, those who were born and lived part of their lives in Lithuania, has now died out. Many of their younger grandchildren live abroad. No one smokes any longer and no one drinks very much because Midnight Mass is at ten instead of midnight, and even so that is too late for those who want to go to bed early and go to Mass the next day. For some, it's the only Mass of the year. These days, many skip it altogether.

The number of dishes has fallen because people want to watch their weight. We invite friends to help fill the places of the those who are gone, sometimes Jews who are our friends and look with kindness upon the traditions that still remain.

But I wanted above all here to write about the Kūčioses of the past, very much influenced by our parents, who brought their refugees' pain and Lithuanian traditions with them, adapting them as their children became more and more Canadian. They are gone now, and those moments are gone: the smell of cigarette smoke and the way it stung my eyes, the smell of rye and ginger ale, and the loud and boisterous stories that we all told, even if no one was listening, on those long gone Kūčioses of the past.

five
The Endless (Lithuanian) Summer (Camp)

LITHUANIAN SUMMER CAMPS DOTTED NORTH AMERICA and came in two varieties. The first would be "bible camps" in modern parlance, but this sounds much too evangelical. At the camps I attended we never read the Bible. The closest we got was listening to homilies from the priest. We might have called these places parish camps if we were forced to describe them in English. To say they were Catholic would have been redundant because Lithuanians were, by default, it seemed to us, Catholic, with only a smattering of Lutherans. We knew nothing of Lithuanian Jews.

Even for those parents with cottages, the schools' summer vacations were too long and work vacations too short, and kids hanging around the house unsupervised got into trouble. So we were shipped off to camp, and the first one for me at age ten was around the corner from our own cottage in Wasaga. It had nothing to do with nature and was a sort of sports and choir camp. I was chosen last for baseball and basketball and tried whenever possible to end up in a game that was a variation of dodgeball, because there were no real opportunities to embarrass your own team.

I was equally bad in choir. So much so that the nervous, chain-smoking priest who directed us asked me to stand silently in the back when we sang. When my parents showed up for the concert, I mouthed the words to make them feel good. The choirmaster played along.

Lithuanian summer camp was the kid version of a Borscht Belt resort. We ate in a wooden hall that tripled as lunch room, church, and dance hall, and in those early days of the 1960s the volunteer moms recognized no such things as light summer or Canadian foods. Squeezed in cheek by jowl in atrocious heat, we were served gigantic Lithuanian "hamburgers," actually coarse meatballs the size of baseballs. You could see chunks of bread and onions that had been imperfectly mixed into the meat, which lay in sauce made pale gray by the addition of liberal amounts of sour cream. Hot dogs were recognizably "Canadian," but these were considered a bit light, more a snack food than a serious meal of meat, potatoes, and vegetables.

After lunch, we'd be mustered on the street with towels and bathing suits to be herded in a column two blocks to the beach while singing patriotic Lithuanian marching songs, as if we were soldiers going off to war. At the beach itself we lay about, awaiting the arrival of the "snack car" that might contain jam crepes that had been kept warm by sitting in the hot trunk of an automobile. These were handed to us dripping with jam that ran until our fingers were sticky and covered with sand. We charged into the water to wash them off before marching back to camp later in the afternoon, dazed with the sun and heat, to lounge on our bunks in our stifling barracks rooms until dinner and then the evening program.

This was usually an informal fireside singalong run by the choirmaster. The bonfire itself was open house for other holidaying Lithuanians who sat around on benches with children too small to camp. Then it was games, which might be dodgeball or a bizarre circle game in which someone was picked to chase another kid around the fire while beating him or her with a knotted towel.

If it rained, we had dances in the dining hall, where the boys jostled one another to ask the more popular girls to dance the slow dances, in particular if the girl of interest wore a mohair sweater. To hold hands and be close to a girl was glorious enough, but if she wore a mohair sweater, she was as soft as a rabbit (but you couldn't pet her).

Between choir songs and Lithuanian food, the air was thick with immigrant ethnic atmosphere, but pop culture hovered over us and entered into our hearts and minds. Our favourite song was "House of the Rising Sun" because it was over four minutes long and that was the longest you ever got to hold on to a girl.

Then it was to bed in our bunks in the boys' barracks, like a long old motel with many rooms and four kids in each one, with paper walls through which we shouted jokes and jibes until our camp counsellor, who called himself "The Butcher," came to settle us down for the night.

Parents came to visit on Sundays when Mass was held in the stifling dining hall. Easily a hundred or more fit inside. The back of the building consisted of interlocking doors that swung open so another fifty or sixty could sit on benches outside. And around the front door, as on Christmas Eve, always with arms crossed cockily, stood the Catholic "toughs." Sometimes one of them would smirk, or another whisper, only to be shushed by some elderly person sitting near the back doors.

I'D NEVER BEEN outside the suburbs or Wasaga Beach, and the wilder woods up at Lithuanian Scout camp — dotted with the Shield's pink granite rocks — were a revelation to me. I was a thirteen-year-old greenhorn. At night, I thought the deep sound of bullfrogs down at the lake was really a chorus of drunk Lithuanian men singing in the distance.

Mistaking any sound for a chorus of drunk Lithuanian men singing in the distance reflects one aspect of Lithuanian upbringing. Drunk Lithuanian men might also be singing close by, often downstairs when you were a kid trying to sleep in your bedroom. The drunk men were often in a haze of tobacco, using highballs as the chasers for the more serious drinking of shots. In other words, singing drunk men were more common in my childhood than frogs.

If the Wasaga camp was a Borscht Belt for kids, the Lithuanian Boy Scout camp was like a low-rent boot camp in Muskoka, a woody part of Ontario's Canadian Shield.

For some reason, I ended up in the Lithuanian Sea Scouts, more focused on boating than hiking. Within the ethnic Catholic context, Sea Scouts were slightly disreputable, the hooligans of summer camp. We all owned machetes or bayonets and played chicken with them until one kid actually got stabbed in the foot. I once bent over to tie my shoelaces and an orange flung from fifty feet away found my right buttock. Low-level violence was considered part of the fun. We slept on cots set on wooden platforms inside canvas tents with upturned sides for ventilation. Two of my fellow Scouts, one on each side of my cot, tossed me outside by sliding my cot onto the forest floor one morning before breakfast. They were amused, and even more amused when I reached up to punch one of them in the face, and hit only his forehead, spraining my wrist.

Each tent had a bucket of sand in case of fire, and once we were old enough to smoke, at fifteen or so, the bucket was our ash tray to prevent littering in the woods. Sea Scouts competed with the other Boy Scouts, but we did not usually fight. However, if we managed to capture one of the boys from another unit outside at night, we might tie him to a tree where he'd howl about mosquitos until one of his brethren came to free him.

We had to go to Mass every morning before breakfast, served by a jolly old Montreal priest who could get through the whole thing in under fifteen minutes. The minority Lutheran kids were exempt from Catholic Mass and we envied their lying around playing with folding knives for another fifteen minutes while we sat through our religious service.

In this interval between childhood and summer jobs I learned to canoe and sail and put on skits. The girls were always objects of desire. I tried to kiss a girl on the dark path back to her side of the camp but ended up smearing her ear and was too embarrassed to look at her the next day. There were not enough sailboats, so we were supposed to go out in parties of four, but I managed to get a girl on board with me and sneaked out. But I was nervous and forgot to lower the centre board, so the sailboat drifted aimlessly until a more experienced but younger camper came out in a motorboat to help us. I was mortified. The girl I pined for was not impressed.

Our pleasant shenanigans were played out on Fox Lake, while across the lake lay Camp Winnebagoe, with its many new sailboats, a water slide, and unpatched canoes. Camp Winnebagoe represented Canada to us — English Canada — the place where boats and tents were first-class and kids wore polo shirts with emblems. We did not consort with them in any way, but if we canoed or sailed by their beach, we would enviously admire their fine goods from a distance and console ourselves with working-class-type chips on our shoulders that we were tougher, more authentic, more capable.

All of this kind of comparison was fantasy. I don't know what the Winnebagoe kids thought of us, or if they thought of us at all. But this envy did reveal a bit of an underlying characteristic: a sense of unworthiness of the kind that had made me want to be English when I was a child. Had I had the ability to articulate my feelings, I might have imagined we belonged to the class of carpenters and plumbers, with some doctors and engineers and chemists on the higher end. On their side, they had bankers and politicians, financiers and lawyers. They ruled and we served.

These kinds of unarticulated feelings were just passing clouds that obscured the otherwise warm and sunny times. And besides, the kids I camped with went on to be lawyers and dentists, surgeons and teachers. There was a lot of alcohol in our culture, and it took down some of the boys I camped with long before they reached old age. But alcohol has taken down many, irrespective of their ethnicity. The stigma of immigration went on to be no stigma at all after we got older. It just added another layer to our experience of growing up in this country our parents had landed on, after the shipwreck of Europe in the Second World War.

As for what others had suffered here before the arrival of our parents, it would take decades for that knowledge to sink in.

six

Lithuanian School, High School, and Girls

SATURDAY MORNING LITHUANIAN LANGUAGE SCHOOL was the cruel trick our parents played on their children. If we refused to be liquid wax they could pour into ethnic moulds, parents could nevertheless shape our reluctantly malleable selves another way, and Lithuanian school was the way to do it. My parents decided to wait until enough suburban Lithuanian kids were available to run a rotating carpool to drive us to Lithuanian school in Toronto on Saturday mornings, and as a result, I had to wait until I was in Grade Three in Canadian school to be put in Grade One in Lithuanian school. Kids are sensitive to status, and I immediately hated the school for my having to sit with children two years my junior, to say nothing of missing the Saturday morning cartoons.

I never really understood what noun declension was until much later, in high school when I studied Latin. I just knew my father would make us practise this arcane exercise in the car on the way to Saturday school. I had no idea why he was making us do this, taking a word like

42

"house," which was *namas* in Lithuanian, and making us decline it like so:

Nominative, the subject of a sentence:	*namas*
Genitive, the possessive form:	*namo*
Accusative, the object of the verb:	*namą*

And so on through the cases, to be followed by my father's invitation to repeat the exercise with masculine and feminine forms, singulars and plurals, and their associated multiple adjectives.

It was all a nightmare to me, like having dozens of the periodic table of the elements spread over the language and having to memorize all the possible combinations. I didn't understand what we were doing or why we were doing it. Although I spoke the Lithuanian language with my parents and teachers, I could not fathom the mechanics behind the practice. All I knew was that I often got "the endings" wrong in speech and didn't know why.

No one ever got the noun endings wrong in English. The mysterious apostrophe is about the only part of English grammar that escapes many speakers. Teaching people how to use it has employed a lot of English teachers, and I would eventually be one of them. Add commas, and you had enough material for a semester's program of study.

Year in and year out, I suffered, until my sixth Lithuanian Saturday school year, when I was in Grade Eight in English school. I quit Lithuanian school briefly and would only return if I was elevated to the same year I was in English school. The canny teachers figured it was better to hang on to the uncertain Lithuanian at this cost, and they let me go into a higher grade.

I ENTERED WESTON COLLEGIATE at the tail end of an era, one that felt like an Archie Comics world with cardigans, sock hop dances in the afternoons, restrictions against jeans and long hair, and a marching band that played at the football games. By the time I graduated five years later in 1972, sock hops and marching bands were gone; we wore bell bottoms and long hair. We smoked cigarettes out back of the high school by day and joints by night if we were at a monthly dance. The Vietnam War was ending, and Weston was losing its small-town vibe and feeling more like a suburb of Toronto.

The outside world was rich in events and people, but high school was my real home. My older brothers had left behind a reputation as sportsmen of the first rank, but the only team I ever played on was basketball in Grade Nine, and we suffered the ignominy of losing all nine games in our season. My talents would lie elsewhere.

At first the transition to high school was hard because most of the kids came up through what we called "protestant school," otherwise known as "public school," and we were only a smattering of kids from the Catholic system. We were the ones who furtively crossed ourselves before the obligatory Lord's Prayer at the beginning of the day and refused to add "… for thine is the power and glory…" to the end of the prayer because it was what "protestants" said, not Catholics. We used upper case to define ourselves, but lower case for "protestants" because there was a variety of them and anyway, who could tell one from the other?

We'd grown up in elementary school with the Catholic girls who ended up feeling like sisters, but the high school girls were new, interesting to look at, compelling even. These girls were my main interest, but I was too shy to do anything but clown around in front of them. I was slow to mature. We were a class of artsy kids who would become teachers and lawyers, dentists and businessmen if we graduated, but in our first year the sorting hadn't happened yet. There were a couple of tough kids in the class who persecuted the rest of us. One boy, Nick, who was repeating the year, made himself feel better by pushing the weaker ones around. Influenced by too many westerns and Disney films in which justice triumphed, I pushed back against Nick during math class in a portable and he challenged me to a fight outside between classes. Hundreds of kids were on the move between portables and the main school building.

I asked my fellow artsy students to hold my books for me but discovered they were too frightened to be associated with me in case I lost. Only Jane, one of the fascinating Protestant girls, held my books. "Brain Jane" they called her, both enviously and dismissively, a willow, a girl who would become the most important one to me in my high school life in different ways in different years.

We stood off in the field and Nick shoved me hard and I fell back. Then I stepped forward again. I was determined this would not be a pushing match. I stood for justice and took a swing at him. But I had no experience in fighting. It seemed a hard punch might be too extreme, so I pulled it and landed a glancing swipe on his cheek.

I think I remember the fist with four initial rings coming at me, but maybe it was the imprint they left on my face that told me they had been there. I definitely remember sparks rather than stars, but no pain. Just a strong blow. When my head cleared, I put up my fists and started moving in for the next round. But by then Nick was looking at me in shock and the math teacher had raced from across the field to pull us apart. Hundreds of kids changing classes had stopped moving to watch what was happening. I looked down and saw blood was pouring down from my face and onto my pale blue shirt. I looked like someone who had been shot in the chest.

The nurse stuffed cotton up my nostrils and I rinsed out the blood on my shirt in cold water in the bathroom and wore it sopping wet for my meeting with the vice-principal. I told him my parents couldn't know or they'd make me switch to the Catholic high school. My brothers had gone to public high school because in their day, Catholic high school charged tuition. That was no longer true, but I enjoyed walking in my older brothers' footsteps as much as I could. And besides, Catholic high school was segregated, and I wanted to be around girls.

So the vice-principal had us shake hands and gave us three detentions each. To his credit, Nick said we had bonded now, and he'd defend me in the future if ever I needed it. Back home, my mother seemed to accept my story of a stray soccer ball. At the hospital the doctor said my nose had been broken but not to worry about it unless it grew out crooked, in which case I should return to have it broken again and straightened.

I went back to school the next day and learned that all spoils go to the victor. The artsy boys who I had stood up for fell over themselves congratulating the tough who broke my nose. But not Jane. She looked at me and winced in sympathy at my bruised face. The following year I would kiss her after a party and then not know what to do next. Later we'd do homework together or, more often, she'd help me with mine, and we'd take a break to neck for a while or go out for ice cream sundaes and neck a bit more. Her mother let me know that as a Catholic and an Eastern European, I came from the kind of people who worked as hired hands on her parents' farm. Over the five years of high school, Jane and I were often close, but we ended up being near misses for a serious relationship. Our paths diverged after high school, and she went off to study medicine in California while I stayed behind to study English Literature.

In the following year, with the fight behind me, I became the talker, the variety show actor, the joker, the drama club ham, the student council vice-president, and eventually valedictorian after Jane passed on the honour. Useless in the maths and sciences except chemistry, I succeeded cockily in English and history, declining to prepare seriously for presentations because I knew I could wing it better than most hard-working strivers. I represented the school by phoning in local hockey scores at the Toronto Telegram newspaper and was given a suit as the school's rep at the Simpson's department store.

I did well within narrow boundaries and terribly beyond them.

Doctor Mambourg, the chilly German teacher — "Sileika, faulpelz, stehen sie auf!" — challenged me to stand and say something intelligent about the 1970 October Crisis in Quebec and Pierre Trudeau's controversial invocation of the War Measures Act. Poor at German grammar, I ran an extemporaneous monologue on Canadian politics in English, and then responded to his questions at enough length to fill the class's allotted time. The doctor admired my rhetoric but told me I was doing the right thing when I dropped the class at Christmas after getting a mark of forty-seven per cent. I had been beguiled into German class by Jane, forgetting she was very smart and anyway spoke German at home.

During two of those summers, between factory jobs, I took my extroverted personality into a travelling children's theatre troupe, in which the director presciently put me in the role of a comic wizard. We crammed into a cargo van, sitting atop our disassembled stage, and spent nights in kids' summer camps after putting on our show. More than one camp director looked at us suspiciously and we were given campgrounds on the edge of the properties. I was in love with one woman one summer and another the next, but true to form, I could never get past the "love you like a brother" category. I felt like the clown Pagliacci, laughing on the outside but crying inside. Maddeningly, the actors were relaxed about their bodies and when we were at swimming holes, the women tended not to wear tops. These were supposed to be my sisters, so why couldn't I stop looking surreptitiously at their breasts? I transferred my repressed sexual energy into physical humour.

High school in Ontario ran for five years at that time, and I found my place there happily. It eventually became clear that I was useless not only in maths and sciences but in French too, subjects which acted like sandbags, weights on my academic balloon.

For the longest time, I thought much more about girls than my academic subjects. I secretly fell in love with one girl after another — Jane, Mary Jane, Dianne, Sally, and more — yet I was somehow incapable of acting decisively enough to secure a girlfriend. The lack of a girlfriend troubled my secret self, but it was not something I talked about, especially not with my buddies. In private, I felt as ugly as Cyrano de Bergerac, and passionately passed on the book to girls, none of whom seemed to get the message of that text. Among them, I was the clown who kept passing around a book about a man with a long nose.

But there were other girls who were easier to talk to in the parallel world I inhabited, the secret world outside of my home and the walls of my high school.

FOLK DANCING PLAYS a bigger role in some cultures than others, and as soon as you cross the Oder River heading into Eastern Europe, you enter a zone where dance is as much an expression of patriotism as any national anthem. Add the sport of basketball to Lithuanian folk dancing, and you already have two pillars of its ethnicity. Add a fondness for beer and you'd have three pillars upon which a nation could stand.

I never developed a taste for beer. I was a failure at basketball. And although folk dancing itself did not interest me, I would do almost anything to hold hands with girls and put my arms around their waists. This was a reward that came to me when I was thirteen and was pulled into the Lithuanian Sea Scout Folk Dance Ensemble.

Part of me winces to this day at the goofiness of this name.

My "English" side remembers the "ridiculous" Polish accordion hours that used to be broadcast on TV out of Buffalo, filled with jolly overweight performers with accents.

For a certain type of Brit, some of whose attitudes I assimilated in my Anglophilia, if the "wogs" begin at Calais, the "wogness" increases as one goes east across Europe.

East of Germany is terra incognita for most Westerners, with the potential exception of Poland, which was the inspiration of the reprehensible Polish jokes of the 1960s and '70s, themselves a derisive expression of anti-wogness.

Churchill once said, "From Stettin in the Baltic, to Trieste in the Adriatic, an Iron Curtain has descended across the continent."

Some form of that still exists. What lies beyond Poland, from Tallinn to Sofia, from Minsk to Zagreb, might as well be *Borat*-land, the somewhat ridiculous, somewhat stupid, somewhat primitively violent antisemitic hinterland, provincial and more than provincial — pure hick.

A reviewer of one of my books called my attitude toward all things Lithuanian "ambivalence," and to some degree the reviewer was right. My Canadian side, my English side, was steeped not only in the rolling vowels of Dylan Thomas but also in the romance of English writing, the rush of Jack Kerouac, the Westchester of John Cheever, the Las Vegas of Hunter S. Thompson, the coolness of Mavis Gallant's Paris, the wit of Dorothy Parker at the Algonquin Round Table, the cynicism of John le Carré's Circus in London.

I would eventually find other writers who chided my arrogant English side. Writers who considered those who use the term wogs to be fools untutored in history and life experience.

But all of this came later, after the girls of the Lithuanian Sea Scout Folk Dance Ensemble. I was embarrassed, but at the same time I loved being a part of that ensemble; beyond choirs, there was so little coed activity in those times that the touch of a girl's hand was like electricity, enough to cause near-permanent erections that were exhausting and painful. But they were unnoticed by anyone because no one looked at another person's "privates" in those innocent days and if they did, they assumed you had something in your pocket.

The tactics of our immigrant parents only became clear to me much later, when it turned out to be obvious that if you force boys and girls and young men and

women to be together in their youths, they might pair
off and keep up the national traditions. For small nations
like the Baltics, every individual was a precious national
asset.

IF THE TRAINING in Lithuanian school was boring at first
— all language and songs and folk tales and myths — it
became more interesting as time went on. In particular,
there were the war stories, which were so different from
the war stories we heard in Canadian classrooms.

On TV and in school, the war was a lot like a children's
story with good guys and bad guys. Germany and Japan
were very bad, and Italy kind of bad, and the rest of us
were good guys who prevailed in the end. We knew about
the Holocaust, but only slightly, as a historical tragedy in
a whirlwind of information, like the pages of a calendar
flying off in an old black and white movie.

It was confusing to us, when we were small, that our
parents had all fled to Germany at the end of the war.
Weren't the Germans the bad guys? I can't remember
ever being taught about the Soviets in Canadian school,
except as a mention of them as allies, helping us, and
therefore in the category of "good guys."

None of this fragmented and partial Eastern European
story was taught to us in school when we were young.
It was never mentioned in Canadian school, where our
Grade Nine history text was called *Our Island Home* (in

other words, Britain), and we had to learn the names of all the kings and queens. I learned about what happened in Eastern Europe only in Lithuanian school.

With one exception: the Churchillian story of the Iron Curtain. We saw ads on TV for the Voice of America, with huddled and fearful men holding ears close to radios. Even as a small child I knew the Curtain encircled a kind of prison that contained my cousins and uncles and aunts and even one grandmother, who wrote a letter to my mother regretting she could not buy candy for her grandson. In my mind, when I was small, I envisioned a woman in a headscarf barred from the candy counter at Kresge's, where cinnamon hearts and humbugs and Scotch mints were sold by the pound.

As I grew older, the carrot side of the attraction to things Lithuanian — the attraction to girls — grew stronger, even as my clownish approach to them persisted. I graduated to another, more professional folk dance group with which I danced at events at Toronto's City Hall, ethnic festivals, and sometimes as cheap entertainment at industrial events like the General Electric Annual Summer Picnic at the head office on Dupont Street in Toronto.

We had a tough teacher who wanted us to be semiprofessional. Much was expected of us, but there were many rewards. No longer the shy boy and still in love with girls as a category, I acted cool. I chatted with young women while sharing dressing rooms as if I were a professional performer. Our group scored a trip to Europe, where we got to dance our dances from London to Stuttgart, from Paris to Innsbruck.

The Lithuanian girls were easier to hang out with because their otherwise suspicious and protective fathers gave us easy access by virtue of our ethnicity. One evening in Rochester, a drunk father stuck his head into the room where half a dozen of our dancers were having drinks, and he encouraged us to "mix it up" with sleeping arrangements that night in order to make more Lithuanian babies. His horrified wife beat him with a slipper and he retreated, grinning mischievously.

As to the stick of Lithuanian school and all its aggravations, I was beginning to lose any sense of a stick at all. I was getting interested in the history of this invisible place that my people came from.

seven

The Death of Tony

IF BELONGING TO WHAT USED TO BE CALLED IN CANADA an "ethnic" community can seem like a kind of insularity, a kind of small-town retreat within the big city, a refuge from the massiveness and confusion of "mainstream" urban life, it also brings a kind of cosmopolitanism, a diasporic life, a sense of a parallel world existing close by.

It's also like membership in a secret club. Since I was not a member of a visible minority, I could pass for any kind of white European or American, but those of us in the club had a certain sign by which we recognized one another. Not exactly a Masonic secret handshake, but still something. On the highway, I might see someone with the heraldic symbol of Lithuania, a knight on horseback, pasted discreetly on a window or on a sticker above the license plate. We'd give a beep to one another when passing or look closely through the window to see if it was someone we knew.

And this club had branches in cities all over Canada and America, from Chicago to Boston, Montreal to Detroit, Hamilton to Worcester. My brother, Andy, was ten years older than me and he had been a Lithuanian student activist in his day, driving to summer camps and conferences in all of these cities and others. He was like a diplomat, an ambassador, an envoy, albeit of a poorer country that could not afford hotel rooms. Still, he could travel and always find a bed or a couch in the house of a friend or a relative of a friend all over North America.

Since I emulated my brothers, I wanted to be a diplomat too. And so when I entered university, I became simultaneously more English (though not quite yet Canadian — that would come later) and more Lithuanian.

University let me escape from sciences and maths into a world where I was a vessel longing to be filled with words, but getting there was a close call.

In my final year of high school, taking the one obligatory course of math, I was stymied by a question on the final exam. I knew it was an important question because it had many blank pages stapled in after it. I didn't know what to do with the problem. It wasn't an equation. What was it? I left it blank.

My final score in math in Grade Thirteen was thirty-seven per cent. Although my high marks in English and history would get me into university, I still needed to pass all my other subjects, and I hadn't passed math. I appealed to the sympathetic teacher, who knew me well. He gave me a fifty, a bare pass, on the condition I promise never to study mathematics again.

"You want to go to the University of British Columbia?" my father asked, arms held up and apart as if he were a patriarch faced with an astonishing misfortune, like the birth of a goat from the womb of a cow.

He held his pipe in one hand as he glanced over at the TV playing the news. He loved the news. He lived for the news. His life had almost been destroyed by the war and he kept his ear close to the ground in case fresh disasters were on the horizon. His anxiety had almost been proven reasonable a decade earlier during the Cuban Missile Crisis, when all of us seemed to be on the brink of annihilation. On the other hand, what good would it have done to hear about impending doom on the news? My parents had kept tinned food in the basement in case nuclear war started, but I wasn't sure where they expected to flee to if the mushroom cloud sprouted above us.

I thought my father would be so distracted by the news he might let me slip away unnoticed to UBC. Instead, he was just irritated by the interruption.

"What are you going to study again?"

"English literature."

"And they don't teach this at the University of Toronto?"

"They do, but it's not the same."

I could almost read his mind. On TV, people were dying in Vietnam, and here was this spoiled Canadian man-child, unaware of how entitled he sounded.

"'Not the same, not the same.' I'll tell you what's not the same. The cost. You have a roof and food here. You want me to spend money for another roof and food somewhere else? Out of the question. Forget about it." He put the pipe between his teeth and concentrated on the TV screen.

It was impossible to argue with my father. I couldn't work on him to wear him down. His positions were like the Matterhorn — frigid and immovable.

It may not have been Vancouver, but in the end the downtown Toronto university campus thrilled me just by being downtown. I'd come from a quiet suburb but here was gritty Yonge Street with its massage parlours, a basement cafe with chessboards, and the Club Manatee, a gay club. Back out in the suburbs we didn't even know those kinds of places existed. I wasn't gay, but I could let drop to my suburban friends the nature of that club and feel like a sophisticate, wise to the real ways of the world. It wasn't Vancouver, but maybe better after all. It was all the allure of "downtown." The place was "edgy," just what a young aspiring literary man was looking for.

The University of Toronto is made up of seven affiliated colleges that mostly arose from its religious past. It was my reflex to apply to St. Michael's Catholic College. My older brother had gone there, so I was continuing to emulate his moves. I wasn't in the least religious, but I had grown up with nuns and priests and was comfortable with them, and it turned out most of my peers felt the same way. On campus, I kept tripping across Lithuanians my age at a rate far higher than in any public place I'd ever been to before.

Catholics and Lithuanians, aging hippies and street punks, American draft dodgers; nearby Chinatown and the remains of the old Jewish neighbourhood at Spadina and College, where I ate knishes for the first time. It was a vibrant mash-up and it was intoxicating.

Lithuanian kids I'd known from summer camps and Boy Scouts, folk dancing, and hanging around with my parents' friends made up a few dozen fellow slackers killing time between classes at the university. Some of them could always be counted upon to be sitting in the lounge in St. Michael's College's Brennan Hall, smoking cigarettes and waiting for someone to say something witty. The more serious science types tended to stick to the other end of the campus, but we humanities Lithuanians rubbed shoulders with our lounging Irish and Italian counterparts.

My friend Ramune was a couple of years ahead of me and reigned as the queen of this circle, a wit herself, one who could slice you to shreds if you were boring. She reminded me of Lauren Bacall. Fast with the pen, funny and cynical, at heart she was a journalist and would go on later in life to edit the Toronto Lithuanian newspaper. She had a best friend named John, a different kind of journalist: a sportswriter working full-time for the *Toronto Sun* while simultaneously studying full-time. He always wore a trench coat so he looked like someone from Frank Sinatra's generation. John was our sophisticate. Having flown in from a hockey game in Chicago, he might meet Ramune and a few others at The Bull and The Bear in the Sutton Place Hotel. This bar was not at all for students. It catered to businessmen and achievers, but John was our adult so we fit in if we were with him.

I was fresh out of high school, and although these people were only a couple of years older than me, they felt like real grown-ups whereas I was still in transition. John made sardonic observations, obviously in English. Ramune made cracks in Lithuanian. This was not exactly the Algonquin Round Table, but I had to have my wits about me to keep up.

Out in the broader university world, we were the generation that just missed out on the summer of love, the ones who saw no flowers in anyone's hair, just crushed petals underfoot and empty bottles from the party of a few years earlier. The university newspaper was still radical, calling for strikes of various kinds, but for those of us smoking cigarettes in Brennan Hall, it was mostly just noise.

If once there had been "red diaper babies" from a prewar generation of working-class leftists, those of us whose parents had come from the broad swath of land east of Germany were raised in Churchillian conservatism while steeped in the idea that Churchill and Roosevelt had betrayed us all at Yalta. Not that this entirely formed our worldview. But leftists among my cohort were practically non-existent.

Someone told me there was an annual conference of Lithuanian students, in Cleveland that particular year, and various clubs from various cities would attend. But there was no Lithuanian student club at the University of Toronto. I wanted to go to the conference — Cleveland was just a name to me, but at least it was a destination. It was *away*. Maybe not so hot as Vancouver, but still *away*.

So began my four intense years of Lithuanian student activity while I was simultaneously developing my English side by learning how to read poetry in Old English, a kind of challenge for students who thought Chaucer's Middle English might be too "easy."

The politics of these student conferences had much to do with the situation of Lithuania and other countries that had been swallowed up behind the Iron Curtain. Lithuania in particular, like Poland, relied on the Catholic Church for support and resistance, so there was a strong Catholic element to the politics. For people from these vanished nations, and their children, the Soviets and all communists were the enemy to be vanquished. Some of the families I'd grown up with had left behind babies because parents never intended to be gone for long, so the occupation of the east by the Soviets was not just historical to us. It was real. Now.

In intellectual and academic circles, much early-1970s discourse was still dominated by the New Left. Not only that, but I was studying English, a kind of artsy pursuit, and artsies skewed left in their politics. My English literature colleagues, as well as students of film and theatre, art and art history, were part of this lefty crowd. They supported California grape pickers and opposed South African apartheid and the deteriorating state of Rhodesia.

I had these sympathies too, but the invasion of Czechoslovakia in 1968 had had more resonance for me than the Parisian student uprisings of the same year. I couldn't even really understand what the Parisian students were against, unless it was their parents, and what was so new about that? In my circle of unhyphenated Canadian friends, if you did talk politics, you did not talk about being anti-Soviet. It would have been in bad taste. It would have been like identifying with our parents, with men still wearing fedoras and women living life according to the rules of Betty Crocker: in other words, conservatives.

The reverse prevailed among the Lithuanians, who were indeed conservative, the children of immigrants whose parents had once been lawyers and bureaucrats and now found themselves working in factories. I was uneasy in each camp. At a Lithuanian student party, I confessed I had once voted for the NDP, Canada's social democrats, and the announcement was broadcast across the room to the horror of all those present. To their credit, they did not treat me like a pariah, but like someone who had caught a particularly unfortunate disease.

So sometimes, inhabiting two worlds did not lead to parallel lives, to distinct separation, but instead led to worlds in collision.

I was in my glory in the study of English, although surprised by the revelation that its literature began before the first millennium and ended with Hemingway, who had died a decade earlier. For me, this was too early and too early. The recent decade was exactly the period I was interested in. What about contemporary literature? And by this I did not mean Canadian literature, of which I was largely ignorant. I thought mostly of American writers like Saul Bellow or John Updike, although even then, in my obliviousness, I began to appreciate Margaret Atwood and Robertson Davies.

The two writers who spoke most directly to me were Graham Greene and Joseph Conrad. Graham Greene's realism appealed to me. "Innocence is like a dumb leper who has lost his bell, wandering the world, meaning no harm." Greene seemed to speak of *knowingness*, that the world was not as it seemed, and that well-meaning people could be dangerous. A student of English literature has little spare time because the reading lists are so long, but I ate up the works of Graham Greene and then jumped off from Conrad's *Heart of Darkness* to find every book of his that was still in print. I read *Nostromo* from end to end four times because it too depicted a world in which the best of intentions and the firmest allegiances all went awry.

The two living geniuses of literature at the University of Toronto at the time were Northop Frye at Victoria College and Marshall McLuhan at St. Michael's College, but I was not motivated to study with them. I didn't want theoreticians — I wanted literature as literature. But I was also too ignorant about them. I didn't know what I didn't know. I would come to Frye and the Bible on my own later in my life.

In my first semester I strutted like the high school literary genius I believed myself to be, and when an English prof gave me a C+ on my first essay, I felt it was important to visit him in his Harry Potter–like office in the neo-Gothic University College. "You probably don't realize who I am," I said with full cockiness, and to his credit, this sardonic Australian did not laugh but took a little time to explain to me that high school English stars were all together here now and I would need to learn how to compete with the best. He gave me a few tips and I went away a little humbled, a little more educated, but not quite entirely modest about my talents. I did eventually learn enough from him and others like him to graduate with honours a few years later.

At the end of that first year, I visited him again to alert him that I had been accepted into a creative writing course at Victoria College. Urbane as ever, he asked on what strength of writing I had been admitted, and when I told him there were no writing requirements, he pointed out I had been admitted on the *expectation* of talent rather than the *demonstration* of talent. I nodded in agreement, not quite realizing just how funny his statement was.

David Knight was an astonishingly generous English professor at Victoria College who had so many applicants for his creative writing class that he split the group in two and ran a supplementary class to make sure all those who wanted to get in could do so. We'd meet on Thursday evenings for three hours in a boardroom to read each other's work and talk about it. This was my introduction to the study of creative writing. Those of us in that illuminated boardroom shining out onto the dark campus on winter nights loved every moment of it, as I found out years later when we reminisced about the class.

Learning to conjugate Anglo-Saxon verbs required discipline (so much like declining Lithuanian nouns!) and reading *Paradise Lost* required a dangerously high intake of coffee. Those forms of English were fine. But better was sitting in that room with the wraparound windows showing the zooming-by car headlights on Queen's Park Circle at night. There we wrestled with each other's texts, and the effort was bracing.

Those nights took me deeply not only into the language but into human character as well. We had the poet who told us we didn't have the right to criticize his work. We wondered what he was there for. We had the glamorous TV writer, an older man in a suit, who wanted to write a novel. My colleagues at the table pointed out that I kept coming back to "ethnic" tales in my writing, something I was barely aware of. Over all of us presided the deeply eccentric David Knight with his very long pony tail and Nehru shirts and pendants, like a middle-aged hippie who had never given up the garb.

His language was digressive and funny and I think we provided an outlet for him as well. His one published novel, *Farquharson's Physique and What It Did to His Mind*, was savaged in the *New York Times*, but he was determined to keep on writing novels, and he did.

He took us seriously but would criticize us thoroughly and this was a new experience for us — to learn to take it and make the writing better. One night we retired to the Victoria College residence of one of the students — I remember a coal fireplace that seemed so strange and elegant to me — where we had a case of beer and we'd throw in a quarter for each one we drank. A serious moment descended on the group when someone asked if David saw the potential in any of us to become serious writers. He looked around the room at our faces, thought for a moment, and then said, "Yes, I think one of you might become a real writer. But I can't tell you which one."

Such a wise man. Each of us left that evening knowing we were the anointed one he had thought of but could not name for fear of insulting the others.

David's life and his class were never separate, and we'd meet in his house to decorate his Christmas tree or to look at a new collection of collages by his ever-joking wife, known as ML. With a bum hip, she moved slowly and rocked from side to side as she walked, but this style just seemed to make her jokes funnier. Laughter and irony ruled that house, as well as a certain refusal to quit any task deemed worthy. When no one would publish David's writing or the work of others he thought worthwhile, he created his own publishing house called Childe Thursday to print the books himself.

That publishing house was named for the Thursday evening classes that would eventually evolve into a permanent coterie of the class's survivors. And I worked with him and my other aspiring writers all the way into the early 1980s, until I became involved with the literary journal *Descant*.

English literature, English essays, English all the time. Whenever I needed to get any serious academic work done, I would go across the street from Brennan Hall to St. Michael's library, which had good soft chairs for reading and good secluded carrels for getting work done. I'd smoke and think and write, practicing an academic version of my later writing life. But when I needed a break, I'd wander the building.

In the card catalogue, there was not one single title with the word "Lithuania." I would go to the stacks where histories of Europe were shelved, and there I would begin to look at the indexes, searching for the elusive word. If I had once been uneasy about the absence of that country on any map, it now became clear the place was practically invisible in the library too. The place that I was so insistent upon hardly existed anywhere.

When the word Lithuania did turn up in a book of European history, the mention was fleeting, or even dismissive. One book claimed that the largest European country of the fifteenth century, Lithuania, had only expanded because the Mongols were so weak. In other words, the country did not really deserve to be so big -- it just lucked into the bad luck of others. Another history, dealing with the interwar period, referred to Lithuania as a "comic opera country."

I was no longer a child, but I was still stung, standing with an open book in the weakly lit stacks in the St.

Michael's library. There was no one else there to share this shameful discovery with me. Maybe no one else would find it shameful. I felt even worse than if the place had been unmentioned. I had often thought I came from a place that did not exist. I was *nobody* from *nowhere*, but that was better than being from a comic opera state, the Fredonia of the Marx Brothers' movie *Duck Soup*.

I'm not sure I articulated it to myself at the time, but in retrospect, I needed to be *someone* from *somewhere*. I had some idea about how to take care of the first part of that equation. I had no idea what it might be possible to do about the second, but history would come to my rescue in a series of events that would have been impossible to imagine at the time.

BACK IN MY ENGLISH CLASSES, David Knight was not the only hero. There were so many good teachers: Father Claude Arnold, who licked his lips so frequently I began to count the gestures and arrived at over a hundred in each class. He invited those of us interested to come one evening to a reception where he would play rare recordings by the last known castrate. Father Madden held his classes in his office, where I remarked that Alexander Pope used a lot of clichés in his poetry. Earnest and kind, Madden gently instructed me that the phrases Pope used were not clichés — Pope created the turns of phrase that thousands quoted to make them into clichés. Gino Matteo was a young Shakespeare scholar who believed we only got to know the master's work by acting it and filming it, and I played the deliciously evil Richard III. Sister Mary Arthur, tough as a street cop, read Anglo-Saxon poetry with such relish you'd think she was seeing it for the first time. A British history professor taught one of those introductory history of history survey classes so well that a couple hundred of us gave him a standing ovation at the end of his last lecture. Fred Flahiff considered the moral complexities of the characters in Victorian literature like a combination psychologist and investigating prosecutor. Mrs. Orwen's information on American literature was good if only I could get over her droning voice—I'd say "Concentrate!" to myself. "She *sounds* bad, but she *is* good."

AT THE SAME TIME, I was dashing around working with my Lithuanian student club. I dated a Lithuanian girl (finally a girlfriend!) named Giedre. After all, who could put up with all this Lithuanian activity unless part of the same team?

One of Giedre's friends, from Boston, was a kind of Lithuanian hipster, if such a thing was even possible, one with a Fu Manchu moustache. This projectionist of European art house movies came up for a visit and joined our circle of Lithuanian smokers and wits in Brennan Hall.

Lounging, reflective, he exhaled smoke and studied the end of his cigarette. "Why do they call you *Tony*?" he asked me.

Brennan Hall's common room was an otherworldly place. Sometimes students would skip classes to spend the whole day there, dawdling. There was a piano in the corner but singalongs were rare. The low lighting encouraged indolence. I also played poker in the back room with an assortment of low-stakes gamblers who belonged to their own world, neither academic nor Lithuanian, but now it was this Boston visitor who had me in his sights.

"Why *not* call myself Tony?" I asked.

"It's an English name."

"That's right. Antanas is too hard for most people. Anyway, it means the same as Anthony, so who cares?"

"'Who cares, who cares?'" he echoed. "You come from a tiny nation under threat of extinction, yet you welcome assimilation so easily."

Those I grew up with all used the English versions of their names, and if there were no English versions they made up short forms that were easy to say: Gint for Gintaras, Ramona for Ramūnė, Andy for Audris and so on. We dropped the diacritical marks, so in English documents my last name, Šileika, did not have a tiny V above the S.

Our Boston friend did not stay long, but his comment stuck. I brooded and brooded on it. I thought how I had wanted in my childhood not only to speak and read English, but to *be* English. I'd found out it was a club I could not join. And why would I want to, anyway? If I wasn't going to be some sort of colonized anglophile fool, like the naturalized Pole in John le Carré's *The Looking Glass War*, I would need to establish myself as what I was before I could establish myself as what I wanted to be — namely, a writer.

These thoughts multiplied and built their own pressure, like steam in an enclosed tank. I had to let it out somehow. I marched over to the registrar and insisted that all my student records be changed from "Anthony" to "Antanas."

So the transformation began. I informed all of my friends not to call me Tony any longer. Some thought it foolish and wouldn't play along, but I was stubborn enough not to respond if they addressed me with my old name.

I told them Tony was dead and would no longer reply to their greetings.

One of my brothers was born in Lithuania and the other in West Germany. Only I was born in Canada, yet I was the one who insisted on going back to the name that I was christened with, and then going to the bother of changing my name on my passport, because my parents had anticipated making my life easier by registering my birth with the English version of my name.

But this new self did not reject English literature or the English tongue. After all, it was my strongest language. For all my doggedness about my heritage, I spoke Lithuanian indifferently and could barely write it at all, having snoozed through most of the grammar lessons of my childhood. I could be Lithuanian within the framework of English literature and the English language, a situation that would bemuse Lithuanian literary critics in that country four decades later.

To this day, there is an irritating former high school acquaintance who, upon sighting me, likes to call out the name Tony as loudly as he can. The greater the distance between us, the higher his volume. "Tony! Tony! Tony!" His message is very clear, a version of Alice Munro's title, *Who Do You Think You Are?*

I let the irritation pass. It matters less now. Antanas is not so unusual anymore, when we have immigrants from so many countries with so many names that are new to us. I tell people it's simply a dyslexic version of "Santana."

IN A WHIRLWIND of frantic ethnic student bustle, in 1975 we organized a Lithuanian student conference at the Royal York Hotel in Toronto and managed to corral 750 Lithuanians from across North America, mostly students, to hear a brief address by Mayor Crombie. That night, after the hotel closed the doors on our ballroom at midnight, I invited a couple of accordion players and about a hundred students to dance in the lobby of the hotel, with its high dark beams like those of a German castle or medieval mead hall. The management was so eager to contain us that they offered us a party room where we could sing and dance all night, and that was what we did.

And then it was all over. I was nearing the end of my studies. It was time to get serious about literature. I intended to be a writer. The Lithuanian frolic was going to end.

But my new girlfriend also happened to be Lithuanian, and I set off on my English literary future along with a Lithuanian girl who became my wife. She intended to be an artist, so we had aspirations in common.

Of course she "happened" to be Lithuanian. I was knee-deep in Lithuanians, so odds were that any young woman I ended up with would be one too. It didn't feel like it. To me she really was the woman I did just happen to fall for. Actually, I still believe this.

And the rest of all that Lithuanian business? After university, it was going to be behind us. We were bored of it. We would put it aside along with the preoccupations of childhood. We had more important things to do. It never seemed significant to me at the time that she had gone through something like what I had experienced.

Growing up she had used her middle name, Helen, but by university she had changed to her Lithuanian name, Snaigė. And if Antanas was hard for some people to pronounce, Snaigė was a mouthful, and why was there a dot over the last letter in her name? She dropped the dot and stayed just Snaige, because after all, who could even understand what a diacritical mark was?

She would be going off to Paris to study art at the École des Beaux-Arts. I would have followed her anywhere, so I ended up in Paris too. I planned to be a writer and had already spent one year working in the college parking lot booth while waiting for her to graduate. As far as we knew, there were no Lithuanians in Paris, and if there were, we had no intention of looking them up.

However, I offered to take a watch over for the friend of a Lithuanian friend. How important could that be?

eight

Paris

To some, Paris was *A Moveable Feast*, "Babylon Revisited," the haunt of Mordecai Richler and Mavis Gallant. But to dream of a city is one thing. To live in it is another. Our lives were closer to, if not exactly the same as, those of the aspiring artists in Henri Murger's *The Bohemians of the Latin Quarter*, a work that inspired the opera *La bohème*. In that story, the aspiring writer burns his manuscript for heat because his garret is so cold, and the artist sells his painting to a butcher who uses it as a sign for his shop.

I lived on the Rue de Javel, basically "Laundry Bleach Street," in a dreary long-stay hotel with a shower in my vestibule and a counter there where I set up a gas burner on which to cook. The gas burner was useful when the room became too cold; the danger of carbon monoxide poisoning never entered my mind. The toilet was down the hall. My furnished room was a study in rose, from the flowered wallpaper to the bed cover. I had a wardrobe, a small table I used as a desk, and two hard chairs.

The ground floor window opened right onto the sidewalk. When I sat working on my first attempt at a novel, I was only a few feet away from anyone passing by. In the winter dark, when I had not yet closed the clanging iron shutters for the night and my face was illuminated by my desk lamp, passers-by would give startled looks to see someone so near. In the summer, with my window open, we'd practically be face to face. I didn't mind. I sat at that desk for hours going through a slow cycle of coffee, cigarette, chocolate, and finally mandarin orange to cleanse my palette before starting the cycle again.

The novel was based on a train trip I'd taken out of Lithuania to East Berlin a couple of years earlier. The short visit had been a haze of alcohol, too much food, and awkward sentiment with an uncle and cousins. The visit had been the first family contact since the war, over thirty years before. But what had really fired my imagination was the married woman who happened to be in my four-bed train couchette on the Vilnius–Warsaw leg of my trip. We became friendly, and then warm, and she bribed the fat female conductor with a massive slab of smoked bacon my relatives had given me back in Lithuania.

Thanks to the bribe, we were alone in the sleeping compartment overnight from Warsaw to East Berlin, where she was travelling to visit a friend. She was married, I was single. She was from the East, I was from the West. The electricity was intense. Her next train left

Berlin several hours after our arrival, so we spent the afternoon together, wandering East Berlin hand in hand, frequently pausing to kiss, cursing the fate that made us meet only to make us separate.

The train trip had been a feverish romantic reverie. Never mind that my friend Al, whom I met that evening in West Berlin, told me I was an idiot who had fallen for a Soviet honey trap. I denied it. I was in love, for a while. After my passion cooled, at least the memory of it would make for my first unpublished manuscript. On reflection now, the story sounds like something from a Graham Greene novel, so my reading was showing up in my writing.

In the mornings in Paris, the streets smelling of black tobacco and diesel exhaust, I attended French classes, first at the Alliance Française and later at the Sorbonne. Every weekday, on my return to my room on Rue de Javel, I lunched on spaghetti cooked on my bathroom gas burner. Then I'd take a quick nap and spend the afternoon and evening working on my novel, first in longhand and later on a manual typewriter with a French keyboard that Snaige bought for me as a gift.

Banging those keys required force. I was developing muscular fingers and enjoyed the clack of each key as an audible sign of literary progress.

Dark fell early in Paris, and Snaige lived across town in a very cold *chambre de bonne* in the tenth arrondissement.

She attended art classes at the École des Beaux-Arts most of the day and sometimes in the evenings too. We had no telephones, so we needed to plan when and where to see each other.

Sometimes the rose hotel room became too solitary and our next planned meeting was a day or two away. I'd spend forty minutes crossing town to surprise her at her own room, only to find she wasn't home. Thinking maybe she was still at school, I'd cross town to find she had left the École des Beaux-Arts just a while earlier. By then it was pretty late, and she had early classes, but I'd zoom over again to where she was living to kiss her goodnight, having spent most of the evening on the metro going one way and another.

Why were we living apart? Part of it was the romance of writing and doing art solo, of forging our futures separately, and part of it was not wanting to shock conservative parents who were paying for the majority of her costs. I was living on savings that were supposed to last a year, but which would run out in four months.

There were plenty of things to do and see in Paris, but money was tight, and I spent most of the day staring out the window at people walking by on the sidewalk. Then I'd turn to look back down at my keyboard.

When I had worked for a year after graduation in the glass parking shack at St. Michael's College at the University of Toronto, I wrote stories at my desk. It was a great job because no cash changed hands; all I did was wave people in or wave them away, so there was plenty of time to write. But in that glass booth, I was still on campus, where I knew dozens and dozens of people. In Paris, at my desk, I knew only one person, and she lived across town.

Learning to write was turning out to be a lonely process.

Paris sounded romantic, but I hadn't gone there for the city. I was chasing Snaige. She wanted to study in Paris, and although we never planned it, the city ended up forming us both at the beginning of our adult lives. Nude models were regulars for a couple of hours two days a week at Snaige's printmaking atelier, but students hardly ever bothered to sketch them there. It was usually a woman and she usually sat there bored and cold and ignored. It was not the kind of thing we encountered in school in Toronto. Paris habituated us to drinking wine a little sooner in the decade than our contemporaries back home, who still drank mostly beer or highballs. We learned to eat artichokes, a vegetable I'd never even heard of back home. There were many things like that to learn: How to eat. How to speak quietly. How to tone down colours. How to sit at a table for a long time and to enjoy the moments instead of thinking of the next errand or piece of business that needed to get done.

And at the typewriter I learned that I preferred shorter sentences to longer ones, and narrative over lyricism. I was an avid reader of Raymond Carver and would eventually learn I preferred to write about events, rather than plumbing the depths of thought or emotional response in the manner of Anita Brookner.

Paris consisted of the city and my dark pink room, a transistor radio I'd won in a raffle in Grade Seven, Snaige across town, and books and, eventually, the bookstore where they came from. Books were expensive, but fat ones were not more expensive than thin ones, so I'd go down to Shakespeare and Company and assess the thickness of each book to make sure I got my money's worth. John Fowles's *The Magus* was good at over six hundred pages. James Clavell was less literary, but *Shōgun* delivered over eight hundred pages for about the same price. Needing to read all the time, I could not afford to buy books based on literary merit alone.

The bookstore itself was not yet as famous as it would become, but it already had a revolving cast of expatriates, a suitably cranky George Whitman at the front, and an eccentric layout. There was a combination squat toilet and shower on the second floor, which was handy, because cafes wanted you to buy something if you intended to use their toilets.

Literary readings at Shakespeare and Company were free, so I got to see Lawrence Durrell and the beat poet Ted

Joans as well as the down-on-his-luck, aging journalist-turned-poet Jack Belden. He wore eyeglasses repaired with scotch tape and was always eating as much bread as possible whenever I saw him at a dinner, probably because he wasn't getting much food anywhere else. He was an example of what happened if you lived as a bohemian for too long.

There was also the mysterious Nancy Cole, an older American with a sharp 1920s haircut who did one-woman shows based on the work of Gertrude Stein. I saw her in her one-woman show in a matinee when there was also a one-person audience. I ran across her again years later in Toronto, where she told me she was planning to go on to the United States. I eventually thought I'd look her up again. I discovered she'd told someone she was planning to travel by bus in the United States, and no one who knew her in Paris or Toronto ever heard of her again. The BBC did a show about her called *Missing in Austin, Texas*, and so she has remained. Her papers are gathered in Yale.

Just by hanging around Shakespeare and Company, I got to know these people as well as a group of expat writers headed by American Ken Timmerman. Together, we helped him put out our literary journal, *Paris Voices*. This lefty café intellectual would eventually become a Middle East war correspondent, and a double convert — first to evangelical Christianity (while imprisoned by the

Palestine Liberation Organization) and second to very conservative Republicanism.

But all of that came later. At the time Ken was a bearded provocateur, funny, rude, a great cook, and a scold, charismatic to a point until he drove you crazy. People were always walking out on him in the middle of dinners or drinks. One of our *Paris Voices* contributors, an Israeli army vet, charged into an editorial meeting, seized him by his shirt front, and threatened to punch him out. Ken attracted followers because of his high energy and literary drive, but he could offend as easily as he could inspire. Sometimes simultaneously.

I HAD STUDIED ENGLISH because I knew from an early age I wanted to be a writer. Maybe I could replicate the language that had moved me so much in my youth, or, if not the language itself, at least the narratives. As kids we had sat on the lawns on summer nights — our parents let us stay up late if we were all visible under the halo of a streetlight — and there we would tell each other ghost stories. I loved those nights under the halo, and I was just as happy to hear a story as to tell one, and later in life equally happy to read a story or write one or listen to a story that someone wanted to tell me.

For a developing writer, I was in a good place, away from distractions. What distractions there were at Shakespeare and Company were useful literary ones. We held our editorial meetings on the second floor, where there was a big window overlooking Notre Dame Cathedral, which once in a while blazed golden at sunset when there were dark clouds behind it, sharpening the contrast. Always short of cash, after meetings I'd eat at one of the Arab takeouts that served deep-fried buns with sausage and fries inside, or baguette sandwiches with herring and onions. We invited one another to our flats to eat chicken livers, cod, pasta with great frequency, and sometimes sinewy cuts of meat. The cheapest wine came in litre bottles with plastic dimpled lids, but when we wanted to celebrate, we'd buy *vin mousseux* in place of champagne.

SNAIGE AND I WERE SITTING together in my room on the Rue de Javel one evening, having closed the noisy iron shutters early because the hotel owner, M. Lenoir, was not keen on Snaige spending the night in my room. He didn't mind the occasional visit, but he had specified that he was renting the room to a single person, and if he saw her there too often, he'd suspect she might be intending to move in.

Someone knocked on my iron shutters. That was a rare event, but it had happened once or twice before, when someone I didn't know was looking for someone else I didn't know. I pulled back the heavy rose curtains, closed to keep out as much of the cold as possible, swung open the French windows, and then folded back the slats of the iron shutters to see a woman around my age in a winter coat and with long, dark blonde hair looking at me from the sidewalk.

"*Je crois que tu es celui que je cherche.*"

She was using the familiar *tu*, common among winos and beggars, so I thought it was a scam of some kind and I was going to tell her off.

Then she repeated the same sentence in Lithuanian.

I went down the corridor to let her in to find out what she wanted.

JOLANTA'S FORMER BOYFRIEND IN TORONTO had given me a watch to take to her, but I forgot all about it and here she was, months later. I had only two chairs so I sat on the bed and she and Snaige took the chairs. I pulled over my small table and boiled water for tea.

Jolanta told us about her expatriate life and her Parisian boyfriend of Estonian heritage and asked about us. Among our explanations, Snaige and I stressed that we had no interest in the Lithuanian community. We had been up to our necks in community events back in Toronto and were sick and tired of the small-town aspects that being part of that group brought with it. Everyone knew everyone else. Everyone gossiped. In my adolescence, if I held a girl's hand at the Lithuanian summer hotbed of Wasaga Beach, my parents knew about it before I got home for dinner. Back there, in the Toronto Lithuanian community, it was as if we were living in the nineteenth century instead of the post–flower power 1970s.

"This is Paris. It's different here," she said. "You should come. We have lunch once a month."

Lunch was in the basement of the Italianate École Massillon on the Quai des Célestins and it brought together sixty or seventy Lithuanians of a kind I had never seen before. Three of them were artists: the austere and ascetic printmaker Žibuntas Mikšys, who only dated women two or three decades his junior; the affable sculptor Antanas Mončys, who loved to cast peasant-type clay whistles that he'd play for a couple of bars before stowing in his pocket; and the charismatic and powerful painter Pranas Gailius. There were a couple more geniuses who didn't often show, but were around: the semiotician Algirdas Julien Greimas, the gallery owner Vytautas Kasiulis, and the actors Jean-Christophe Mončys and Karolina Masiulis.

This was not your community of immigrants aspiring to suburban homes and gardens. These were whole categories of people I had not been familiar with back in Canada.

From the old prewar diplomatic corps there was the former military attaché Colonel Juozas Lanskoronskis; Petras Klimas the younger, whose father, a signatory of the Lithuanian declaration of independence, had been imprisoned both by the Gestapo and by the Soviets in the gulag; and Ričardas Bačkis, whose father had been a diplomat and whose brother would go on to become cardinal of Vilnius in independent Lithuania. All this company was overseen by the chief of the Catholic Mission, the chain-smoking sports enthusiast Monseigneur Jonas Petrošius.

Much of the food at the monthly Lithuanian Sunday lunch was prepared by aging nuns who had entered convents in France in the interwar period because it was too hard to do so in Lithuania. And among this crew were a few working-class parents, several of whose children were of the same generation as Snaige and me, although none of them spoke much Lithuanian.

This seemed to be an exotic, but fading, community. There had been hundreds at some point right after the war, but most later moved to North America if they could, and only the artistic, eccentric, and political types stayed behind, with a scattering of undefined others and students passing through. John le Carré, who in his work sometimes dismissed the independence aspirations of various postwar expatriates as sad, deluded dreams, would have recognized this crowd immediately, and he might have smiled at our irrelevance in a bipolar world.

Snaige and I loved them all. I fell for their braininess and artiness. We had thought all Lithuanians were something like stolid suburban American Republicans, but these people weren't. They were smart, and those that were not smart had style or charm or appealing eccentricity. Above all, they had lived in France long enough to have profoundly Gallic habits and attitudes.

SNAIGE AND I DECIDED to marry, a very amusing choice to our *savoir vivre* French friends, who found young marriage bourgeois. We agreed to get the job done in Paris.

My father wrote to say we were getting married like thieves in the night and he would not attend because he had never flown and never intended to do so before he died. Having written all that, he wished us well if we went ahead with our plans and ignored his advice. After all, he reasoned, I'd never taken his advice before, so why should I begin now? He sent us a cigarette lighter as a wedding gift, but Snaige didn't smoke.

Monseigneur Petrošius did the honours in L'église Saint-Paul-Saint-Louis, and many of the people named above came to the reception in Petrošius's airy apartment on the Rue des Lions Saint-Paul. Other parents and our brothers showed up, as well as a couple of aunts and a smattering of friends. Our only glitch at that wedding consisted of a pair of my *Paris Voices* American editors who'd offered to take photographs. Having been raised staunch Protestants, they were a little wary of the Catholic altar and kept their distance from it. In their photos, we look like distant dolls on a remote stage.

Outside the church we met a university friend, James Conway, eating a banana on the steps. He was living in Ireland, and we didn't know how he'd found us and decided to stop by. He'd end up years later running an opera company in London.

As we walked out from the church on the way back to the reception, we found it was market day on the Rue Saint-Antoine, and the strawberry sellers had parked their pushcarts on the road against the sidewalk. We walked between them and the shops on the other side, and shopkeepers came to their doorways to call out, "*Vive les mariés!*"

We toured the town as guides to our relatives and took some out to the Folies Bergère because they wanted to see a girly show. Instead of a honeymoon, Snaige took her parents up to Belgium to meet some Lithuanian relatives travelling with a Soviet chamber orchestra, and I took a few of my relatives down to Nice because they wanted to see the Mediterranean. After all, Snaige and I reasoned, our whole life in Paris was a honeymoon.

WE MOVED TO A SHARED APARTMENT just a stone's throw outside Paris, in the working-class neighbourhood of Ivry-sur-Seine. As my art student wife was etching zinc plates in acid baths in our bedroom, her aspiring writer husband was in the next room editing for *Paris Voices* and writing more of his stories. Although we were both there on student visas and shouldn't have been able to work, I had found a job teaching English to businesspeople for a private school in Versailles. It was a twenty-minute ride by train each day, so on the way in I prepared lessons and on the way back I wrote stories. It was amazing how much I could produce in twenty minutes a day.

Aside from our Lithuanians, most of Snaige's friends were French and came from the art school, and most of my friends were American expatriates at *Paris Voices* and Shakespeare and Company. There were so few Canadians that when Boyd Neil, a freelance literary journalist, went looking for some in order to write an article for *Books in Canada* on the fifty-year anniversary of Morley Callaghan in Paris, he couldn't find anyone besides the august Mavis Gallant and me, and all I had ever published consisted of two stories in *Paris Voices*. For lack of other options, he interviewed me, and I answered his questions as best I could. I got stuck when he asked me who my Canadian writer models were. I didn't have any. I had studied English Literature, which meant mostly Brits and Americans, and I still read mostly Brits and Americans. I bluffed my way through with some sort of answer including Margaret Atwood and Robertson Davies, but I was mortified by my ignorance.

I would need to do something about that when we returned to Canada. I had wanted to be English, and had instead taken the English language, but now I was going to learn how to be a Canadian writer. I was going to learn to live in the house of Canadian literature and maybe help to build some corner of it too.

WHY DID WE BOTHER to return to Canada after two years if we were living such an idyll? Part of the answer came from a dinner we had with our *Paris Voices* friend, Ken Timmerman. We were in a restaurant, and he turned to me to ask if I wanted *lardons* on my salad. I smiled and told him he was losing his English after six years in France. Lardons were French, and the English term was bacon bits.

My spoken French was fluent by that point, and although I felt I was in no danger of losing my English, the tiny slip on Ken's part alerted me that I was living in a French world, not an English one.

We had learned in Paris that Lithuanians were not all the same conservative suburbanites we had known. Our parents had simply adapted to the places where they had landed after the disaster of the war. They had thrived however they could, wherever they could.

En route back to Canada, Snaige and I stopped by a Lithuanian conference in London, where we met two men who would open our eyes to another aspect of Lithuania we had never thought about very much until then.

At Wasaga Beach, with a brand new 1958 Strato Chief! The future never looked brighter. I'm seated between my aunt to the left and my mother to the right. Brother Andy is standing.

Šilytus, 1944. Mother and Father with son Audris, on the brink of fleeing before the Red Army. Mom beams over her son, but Father looks pensive.

The shorts, the knee socks, the bow ties! Andy, me, and Joe in front of the Christmas Tree, 1959.

Paris, 1977. I thought of living in this fleabag hotel on the Rue du Bac when I first arrived in Paris. It was a very tight room; we are sitting on the bidet. Where could I settle in to write? I gave it up for the rose-themed room in the fifteenth district.

With the *Paris Voices* team in our upstairs "office" at Shakespeare and Company, 1978. Editor Ken Timmerman is seated, middle. His pregnant wife Monique is on the far left (with the cigarette!) looking at California writer Dan Halford.

Paris, 1978. Snaige wore a white dress to the wedding before slipping into the national costume to carve the pièce montée wedding cake.

Working on my third novel in Barcelona, in 1987, on a very heavy "portable" Kaypro computer — cutting edge technology at the time.

Two handfuls! With sons Dainius and Gintaras in Toronto, Christmas, 1988.

With author Mona Awad at the Vilnius Summer Literary Seminar, 2009. (*Julia Blaukopf*)

In 2019, after winning Book of the Year in Lithuania, I was featured in magazines like this one. The headline reads: "Writers are made, not born."

nine
Two Lithuanian Jews in London

SNAIGE AND I WERE TAKING A SLOW ROUTE BACK TO Canada in 1979. We stayed in a fleabag hotel in London, followed by more stylish horseback riding in the Brecon Beacons in Wales. Having been a counsellor in a summer riding camp, Snaige had experience with horses. I had saddle sores.

Our Parisian Lithuanian friends had asked us to attend a Lithuanian youth congress in London. I wasn't crazy about the idea because, as I have said, I had had too much to do with North American Lithuanians and they were sure to make up the majority of attendees. But the Parisians wanted me to play a role in their stage sketch about the forgotten Lithuanians of Paris, depicting themselves as something like one of the lost tribes of Israel.

The event for a few hundred students took place at St. Mary's University at Strawberry Hill, an assemblage of various types of British architecture and lawns. We walked endlessly upon the many lawns, maybe because they were strictly protected back in France. Snaige and

I had once been arrested for walking on a lawn in Parc Montsouris in Paris.

Those types of conferences tended to touch on the politics, religion, and culture of Lithuania, and the speakers ranged from dreadfully earnest to astonishingly brilliant. I usually sat by an exit door in case I needed to flee a boring lecture after the first ten minutes.

One of the speakers at the congress was a middle-aged man named Aleksandras Štromas, a relatively recent Lithuanian émigré. Short and rotund in a dark suit, with curly hair and thick-rimmed eyeglasses, he talked fast, barely pausing to breathe unless to suck on a cigarette. He carried the implausible message that the Soviet Union was doomed to collapse, that its internal contradictions and shortcomings were unavoidably self-destructive. This was 1979, a time when the Soviet Union seemed unassailable and was about to enter Afghanistan with what looked like high chances of success.

What Štromas had to say sounded beyond implausible. It sounded ludicrous.

The Russian dissident Andrei Amalrik had said the same in 1970 in his essay *Will the Soviet Union Survive Until 1984?* — but none of us in the audience had read Amalrik or even heard of him.

Štromas was charismatic, though I was conflicted about him. I thought that he was a half-baked optimist, notwithstanding his intelligence, his training in law, and his eloquence. I even thought he might have an agenda of some kind, having been put up to convince us of this counterintuitive conclusion. After his talk, I told him I had questions and I had objections. But I was young, and didn't know as much as I thought I did. I think he found my arguments, based on readings no deeper than *Time* magazine, mildly amusing, but he treated me without condescension.

He did not merely explain. He engaged in deep conversation, developing thoughts in paragraphs and subparagraphs that looped back to his main points. I wanted to talk to him some more, or rather to listen to him some more, so I invited him back to my residence room that evening. He agreed and thought I might like to meet his friend, the writer Icchokas Meras, as well. So Snaige and I stocked up on wine and beer, liquor and snacks, and prepared to grill these two men, each on the verge of fifty and each willing to spend an evening enlightening a pair of curious but naïve Canadians.

They came up to our third-floor room with the sloping ceiling, and each of them sat in a hard chair as Snaige and I sat on the edge of a bed with a laden table between the four of us. There was no awkwardness. If you imagine a Soviet kitchen table across which intellectuals and dissidents speak with passion, you will have some idea of what the atmosphere was like. Štromas talked and ate, drank and smoked, and gestured with his hands.

They began to talk about the Soviet Union, but we wanted to know them better, and in the end, they delivered their life stories. Štromas was a Jew whose father was murdered in the grotesque Lietūkis Garage massacre in the opening days of the Holocaust in Kaunas, Lithuania. A group of Jews were beaten to death in public or had flowing water hoses forced down their throats until their bodies burst. A smirking crowd looked on, including a mother with her child, and all of this was documented in photographs. It is one of the ugliest instances of Jewish murder in the Holocaust and recorded in horrific detail in a series of photographs taken by a German soldier.

Štromas's mother committed suicide later while a prisoner in the Stutthof concentration camp, but he and his sister survived the war sheltered by a Lithuanian family. In an unusual twist, Štromas went on to be raised by the chairman of the Lithuanian Communist Party, Antanas Sniečkus, who ruled Lithuania until his death in 1974. Štromas thus suffered terrible family losses, yet was raised with all the privilege of a member of the communist *nomenklatura*, the ruling class.

But the children of the nomenklatura did not necessarily adhere to their parents' generation's ideas. Štromas studied law in Lithuania and Moscow but became a dissident and was forced in 1976 to leave the Soviet Union for Britain, where his sister had settled after the war.

The friend he brought along to our room that night, Icchokas Meras, was elfin and soft-spoken, a sharp contrast to his friend, the big man of big ideas. Meras's story had to do with being led as a seven-year-old to a pit with his Jewish family to be shot during the Holocaust in Lithuania. As this was happening, a Catholic priest rushed in to say that children should not be shot, so they were temporarily set aside. Others would eventually be killed the next day, but Meras was saved by a Lithuanian family. Meras said various families kept him, until one by one they gave him up for fear of being found out by the Germans. He ended up standing on a street in Kaunas and weeping when a passing journalist asked him what was wrong. The child Meras said nobody wanted him, so the journalist took him home and protected him until the end of the war. Meras went on to study radio technology, but he became a prominent writer and had published several novels before emigrating to Israel.

To say Snaige and I had scant knowledge of the Holocaust in Lithuania would have been an understatement. We were raised on the tragedy of our relatives' suffering under the Soviets, and in our circles the Holocaust had been described as a regrettable horror perpetrated by the Germans. We didn't know much about Lithuanian collaboration at all, although it had come up in the television series *Holocaust* the year before.

antanas sileika

And here were two Lithuanian Jews, who had suffered terribly and lost family members, now drinking and generously educating a pair of well-meaning but ignorant young people. Štromas was a great Lithuanian nationalist, whom I would see again in years to come as he attended conferences in the United States. I'd meet Meras repeatedly in America as well. Although he lived in Israel, Meras continued to write in the Lithuanian language.

What amazed me about these two men was their good-natured willingness to spend time with people like Snaige and me, just a pair of youths without connections, without a larger audience. Much later in life, I have been approached by young people of various kinds, aspiring writers or those with traces of lost Lithuanian heritage, always seeking some kind of information or groping for insight that I might help them find. With a day job most of my life and a writing career after hours, I have never had much time to spare, but Štromas and Meras opened the doors of perception for us. Although our life experience has been nothing like theirs, we've learned not to be too busy at times when strangers want to know something. They were an education beyond the familiar community of our Lithuanian parents' friends and their children, and the familiar history of Lithuanian suffering under the Soviets.

This was far from the conclusion of our education in the Holocaust in Lithuania, of the relationship between Jews and Lithuanians past and present. The thorny and painful subject would come up again and again in our lives.

ten
Goodbye to All That

Upon our return to Canada, one of my first acts was to get an unlisted telephone number for our Toronto apartment in the West End neighbourhood of Swansea. My reasoning was the same as it had initially been in Paris. Once again, I swore off Lithuanians. I wanted no dinners, no dances, no conferences, no committees. I needed to clear away the distractions of Lithuanians in order to become a Canadian writer.

Not that I was really aware of a literary world aside from the English one I had studied in university and the romantic one in my mind with no objective correlative in reality. I had published those few stories in Paris, but was now keenly aware of how little I knew about writing in Canada, so I was going to learn.

Snaige considered carrying on her art education by taking an MFA somewhere, but her brother had opened a commercial silkscreen printing company that was starting to boom and he needed help. She dove into this business and managed to keep up her art practice at the same time. She joined Open Studio, a printmakers' collective downtown. Unlike painters, who can work well enough alone, printers require lithography stones and presses of various kinds as well as ventilation to take off noxious fumes. Open Studio provided all the technical material as well as a circle of artist colleagues and friends, some of whom she would continue to show with decades later.

With her income of $150 a week and our rent of $200 a month, Snaige made enough for us to live on. I stayed home to read and write while earning nothing at all.

To educate myself, I went down to Longhouse Books on Yonge Street and spent a quarter of our savings buying every single Canadian literary journal that existed. Since I had learned a bit about contemporary literature while volunteering with *Paris Voices*, I thought I could learn a little more by doing the same here. I read all of those journals, over twenty. I needed to find a journal that appealed to me, a home where I could build my knowledge of Canadian literature and figure out where I fit in.

I narrowed my search to an elegant and compelling journal called *Descant* and wrote to publisher Karen Mulhallen to volunteer. I was more than a little intimidated by the baby grand piano and the wide selection of art hanging on her walls and I was all too aware of my ignorance. She was kind and accepting and agreed to let me join the editorial collective.

Karen later said I did not speak at editorial meetings for about a year. I needed to understand how things worked, and began with the basics. It turned out she needed someone to empty the mailbox weekly and sort the submissions and pass them out to the various co-editors. I also handled subscribers, some of whom hadn't paid for three years, and libraries, some of whose queries we'd never responded to. I was apprenticing. All the busy grunt work was the price I paid for the right to sit around a table with CanLit academics — Russell Brown and Donna Bennett, Karen herself, writer Rosemary Sullivan, lawyer-with-a-literary-bent Gordon Sato, and others over the years — reading submissions or figuring out which prominent Canadian writers from whom to solicit stories to put in our literary journal.

Karen later remarked that although I'd been silent for the first year, after that I would not stop talking. Our editorial meetings always included drinks and were often preceded or followed by elaborate meals. I was learning enthusiasm for all the good things in life, from a well-written poem to a compelling story, from the taste of a fresh new aperitif wine to the scent of previously unfamiliar foods such as lychees and longans, osso bucco and *zarzuela de mariscos*.

I was also looking for writers within some kind of literary scene, so Karen called her friend, the Canadian writer M.T. Kelly, and he introduced me to a small crowd that

attended weekly literary readings at Toronto's Harbourfront. Later it would become the venue of the city's widely
admired International Festival of Authors. Between *Descant* work and hanging out at the nascent Harbourfront
Reading Series downtown, I slowly began to develop a
picture of writing in Canada. And I was developing too,
writing stories that found their ways into other literary
journals. I'd finished an unsuccessful novel manuscript in
Paris, and now I was writing another (unsuccessful) one.

I was getting to know myself, and found I was too
restless to spend the whole day at home writing. Snaige
was willing to support us, but I wanted a day job and
found one teaching English to immigrants at Humber
College. It was similar to what I'd done in France, and
since my parents had been immigrants who'd never
mastered the use of the definite article, I had firsthand
knowledge of immigrant language difficulties. The work
also made me look more closely at English grammar and
sentence structure.

The teaching days were intense, involving a lot of
miming and good-natured cajoling. But the hours were
not too long and there was no marking. I loved the
eccentric teachers I taught with. Most of us were part-
timers, people at loose ends. There were a few full-timers,
and I'd eventually become one too, but in the meantime,
we were individualists and originals who threw parties
and wrote Christmas pageants and organized cafeteria

singalongs for a few hundred adult immigrant students. A couple hundred of them from various cultures broke down in laughter when our teacher and vocalist Bill Newman pointed to me and my colleague Declan to sing the chorus lines of *Under the Boardwalk*, and the notes came out as flat as flat could be.

Some of the teachers wanted more than collegial love. Most of the male teachers were young bohemian gays and kept good-naturedly encouraging me to join their "team." One called in late because he'd been arrested after getting into an argument with a streetcar driver. Another washed his hair in the bathroom sink because he lived illegally in an office downtown. I don't know how he washed the rest of his body. A couple of the women married former students from their classes.

Students tended to buy cologne as gifts for their teachers, and these bottles accumulated until one day we got into a cologne fight in the faculty office that housed twenty of us. The place stank for days after that. Knowing the students would buy gifts that we could not turn down, and not wanting any more cologne or statuettes, I used liquor and cigarettes in most of my English class examples and began receiving only lighters and bottles at the end of every six-week term. My colleagues thought me shameless.

This chaotic and energetic atmosphere would change as the years passed and the linguistics grads and English as a Second Language specialists formalized the educational structures and raised their tone by raising the teaching qualifications. But the early years of the 1980s were the Wild West, and I don't think any of the students were the worse for our lack of academic decorum. Sadly, at least four of my gay teacher colleagues died in the AIDS epidemic, and those losses more than anything changed the atmosphere from optimistically energetic to melancholy.

The immigrants of the time were given six months of English training, and their flow was unpredictable. The Federal Manpower office might announce on Thursday that they had four more classes of new students to be trained starting the following Monday, and there'd be a scramble for teachers.

These students were frequently refugees, from the Vietnamese "Boat People" to Polish exiles to those fleeing political danger in Latin America. In other words, we had rooms of thirty variously traumatized adults, some of whose politics were the opposite of the politics of the others. But we all got along somehow — they adjusting as best they could to life in this place, and we trying to lay down basic vocabulary, language good enough for a doctor to get a job as an orderly or a lawyer to get a job as a cleaner. As for teachers of their own languages, those poor former educators had nowhere to go except as volunteers in their own communities or one of the many obscure and humiliating places that paid minimum wage.

At the end of every working day, I'd pick up Snaige in the used car my brother Joe had given me. I kept patching the rust holes but could never get the filler flat nor the touch-up paint correctly matched. The coloured bumps and blotches made the car easy to recognize at a distance. We would eat dinner early and I'd settle in to write from six to nine each weeknight except Friday, and usually another half day or two on the weekend. Once I was earning a salary, Snaige took a day off from the shop each week to work at Open Studio. I was reading all the time, still with the intellectual hunger of youth, but in Canada I didn't need to buy only fat books. I could buy or borrow anything I wanted.

With two exceptions, the Lithuanian world fell away.

I had always felt my people came from an invisible country, but in 1980, Czesław Miłosz won the Nobel Prize in Literature. This remarkable man spoke and wrote in Polish but identified at least partially as Lithuanian, and now his works were translated into English.

The two nations had once been in a federation as the largest country in Europe. Over time, the Polish language dominated the ruling class of Lithuania, with the native tongue only rising as a literary language much later. (Polish and Lithuanian belong to different language groups. They are not even vaguely mutually comprehensible in the manner that Italian and Spanish might be.)

Miłosz wrote repeatedly about his childhood in Lithuania, his student days in Vilnius (called Wilno in his time), and life in Warsaw, Paris, and finally California. Although he was primarily a poet, I found his prose highly evocative, descriptive of a curious Lithuania: part woodland refuge, part fairy tale, and part site of monstrous massacres. And, in *The Captive Mind*, he showed how writers would sell themselves out for publication and adulation. This book was a strong corrective to any romantic illusions I'd ever had about writers, whom I'd imagined as heroes of one kind or another. Writers, it turned out, could be like anyone else. But some of them, like Miłosz, had both courage and insight.

CzesŁaw MiŁosz was a corrective to my sense of Eastern European unworthiness, the invisibility of my youth. His work was the first indication to me that the Anglosphere I inhabited, and which I was enlarging in my mind to include Canadian writing, was also limiting. To imagine that the best writing in the world appeared in *The New Yorker* or was reviewed only in the *Times Literary Supplement* was a sort of provincialism.

In this period, thanks to the editor Anne Collins, I began to review books for *The Globe and Mail* and other publications and to write magazine stories. Richard Handler brought me in to do a little literary radio work with Shelagh Rogers at the CBC. These forays into literary and magazine writing brought me into the practical no-nonsense world of journalism, where stories were "copy" and it never paid to be too precious about your own work. An editor could cut out chunks if the piece was too long or kill it altogether if it wasn't working.

In this life of literary pursuit, outside of reading Miłosz, the only Lithuanian activity besides family events was a late summer trip I made annually to the Santara Conference in southern Michigan at a crumbling country resort called Tabor Farms. It was a long weekend devoted to Lithuanian topics of all sorts, from literature to history, politics, sociology, and anthropology, and even "happenings" inspired by the performance art of Jonas Mekas. Miłosz had read his poetry there, and Aleksandras Štromas became a regular and Icchokas Meras an occasional participant.

I still thought of most Lithuanian community activity as parish- or Boy Scout–related — all rather dull to me. But at Santara, a wide range of intellectuals attended. They were liberals, not dogmatic about anything except their right to be non-dogmatic. Lectures ran all day in the converted barn, but if you felt like sitting by the pool or playing golf, nobody cared. You might spend your time in the bar, where Valdas Adamkus often served the beer. This was a couple of decades before he left the USA to become the president of newly independent Lithuania.

Literary critics Ilona Gražytė-Maziliauskienė, Violeta Kelertienė, and Rimvydas Šilbajoris brought news of what literature was being published in Lithuania. All three of them, particularly Violeta, indulged me as a "Lithuanian" writer working in English. And fatefully, another of the organizers, sociologist Vytautas Kavolis, would later say to me, "Go write something. No matter if it's in English. We'll translate it and put it in *Metmenys,* our Lithuanian literary journal." The story I wrote for him would become the first in my eventual collection about immigrants to Canada, *Buying on Time.*

Although I could speak and understand the language, and read it as well, I was not able to write it with any ease. Also, initially, I read very little of Lithuanian literature and relied on plot summaries delivered by Santara lecturers to get some idea of what was being written in the country itself.

Snaige and I were mostly through with the Lithuanian part of our lives. We spoke the language to our parents, but we used English between ourselves and with our brothers or any other Lithuanians we'd grown up with. The older generation hammered away at the injustice of the Soviet Union's occupation of the Baltics, but it seemed to us this was a hopeless task, a waste of energy.

eleven

The Lithuanian Language Strikes Back

SINCE SNAIGE AND I HAD LITTLE INTEREST IN LITHU-anians as a group, we didn't have much cause to use the language outside of our parents' houses. We did run into Lithuanians we knew, either on the street in West End Toronto, where most of the Eastern European immigrants lived, or at Wasaga Beach, where our parents' generation bought their summer cottages and had a summer camp and parish.

Our generation shared funny stories about Lithuanian parents who never fully adapted to life in North America. Some adapted too well, the women aspiring to a bronzed and suntanned California look, including the sunglasses, and the men transforming themselves into patrician types: doctors, businessmen, and engineers who drank scotch to distinguish themselves from the poorly adapted immigrant men who still drank rye.

Snaige and I had good jobs and were working well in writing and art, but we were still restless in our youthful skins. We began to talk about living abroad again. Then

Snaige became pregnant, giving birth to our son Dainius in 1984.

As every parent knows, having children changes everything, and in our case, the birth took us more deeply into the family and added an ethnic spin. Living in a big one-bedroom apartment in a flat owned by her great-uncle, we didn't have the space or the money to think of nannies when it came to child care, but business and teaching still needed to be attended to. Snaige came home from the hospital, handed baby Dainius to me, and said she was going into work for a couple of hours. She told me he'd just been fed and that I should be OK.

Very few people with newborns are OK, and we called on our families to help, so much so that most daytime child care and some overnight child care was done by Snaige's mother or mine. Suddenly, we were back deep in the bosom of our families. And we were intensely aware of how much our parents were doing, giving us a kind of free pass to work not only at our day jobs but to do a little art or writing if we had the time and were not too tired.

Grateful to our parents, Snaige and I came to a decision. We would no longer speak English in the presence of our son, and later in the presence of our second son, Gintaras, born in 1988. They were spending most of their preschool daytimes with the grandparents anyway, so that gave the children a basis in the Lithuanian language.

To say the shift in language between Snaige and me was difficult would be an understatement. We were accustomed to discussing world affairs or our work, and now we were hobbling ourselves by slipping awkward masks on our thoughts. As well, I had a tendency to revert to the style of my gruff, no-nonsense father when I spoke Lithuanian.

For all this difficulty, we stuck to our decision, easy at first because we could always speak English when the baby was asleep. It was not so easy when the babies turned into toddlers and then children who were with us all their waking time. We would read to the children in the evenings, always Lithuanian books that helped with the vocabulary of the children and ours as well. We kept a dictionary by the bedside because we often did not know the meaning of the words in the stories we were working through.

While reading the adventures of Baron Munchausen to my sons in their bunk beds one night, I came across the Lithuanian word *titnagis*. I didn't know what it meant and I was tired and hoped the boys would let the unfamiliar word slip by unexplained. But no such luck. Dainius, peering down from the upper bunk, stopped me and made me look it up in the dictionary. It meant "flint," which made perfect sense because Baron Munchausen was a hunter who used a flintlock rifle.

In this manner, we began to raise a third generation

speaking the Lithuanian language in Canada. One thing
led to another. Along with the language came Saturday
morning classes for the children, much like the ones I
had so despised in my childhood, Lithuanian Boy Scout
summer camps, and even Sunday Mass at what the boys
referred to as "The Eating Church," because Lithuanian
potato dumplings and kugel were served in the basement
cafeteria after the service.

Was it inertia or determination that made us replicate our childhoods? Were we making a kind of carbon
copy, fainter in definition because we were no longer
immigrants, just the children of immigrants? Some of it
might have been sentimentality, but some of it was the
sense of a historic mission, to be ready somehow for a
fateful day when the occupied Lithuanian nation might
need us.

We recognized this belief was similar to the belief of
the Jews in a Messiah, who would come, but probably not
soon. Still, it was good to be ready. The Lithuanian Boy
Scout motto is similar to the English one — "Be Prepared"
— but the Lithuanian phrase is slightly different. It calls
upon the kids to be "on guard." It implies being ready to
fight. We never thought much about this until later.

I was not very religious and in childhood had been
bored by religious ceremonies. Still, as an adult, I had run
into a man at a conference who described how his parents had no religion and so he went seeking it for himself

and discovered Evangelical Christianity of the Southern USA variety. He told me that Jesus was "the engineer in the choo-choo train" of his religion, and he was pulled along in one of the cars behind. One shouldn't blame Evangelicals for the statements of one adherent, but I found the image so infantile and ludicrous that I decided our children must be given conventional religion.

Lithuanian Catholicism carried a different meaning from Canadian Catholicism because in Soviet times it meant resistance to the communist overlords, much as in Poland. One resisted tyranny in Lithuania by being a Catholic, and the only really successful underground press in Lithuania belonged to the Catholic Church. So while Catholicism was conservative in Canada, it was radical in Lithuania, the vehicle of potential freedom.

Catholicism, for better or worse, joined the Lithuanian language as one of the three educational foundations for the children. The third was music, in the form of the piano lessons and practise that were to go on as long as the children were in elementary school.

I knew that the children would likely reject some elements of this upbringing, so I insisted on the three foundations without the illusion of their permanency. Which was just as well, because children end up going their own ways, and both of our boys did, taking some of what we gave them in their childhood and adapting or abandoning other elements.

The Lithuanian part of our lives was decidedly domestic. Meanwhile, the artistic parts of our lives were eked out as best we could manage in a systematic way. Snaige and I split up the week of evening child care. I had two nights to write and she had two nights for art. We took offices downtown to have space to work in. Friday nights were family nights. Each of us had half a weekend day as well.

The plan was excellent, but it didn't take fatigue into account.

I recall frequently sitting in my car on a weeknight on King Street back in the 1990s, when parking was free after six, waiting for the hour to strike so I could leave the car below and go up to my office to work on some writing. I might be eating a submarine sandwich in the car or saving it to take up to my office. I did not dare close my eyes for a moment because I knew I'd fall asleep if I did. Up in the decrepit but cheap office I rented in those real estate slump days, I'd make a cup of instant coffee and get to work on another story or third attempt at a novel, trying to write my way into a literary life that went beyond editing and writing book reviews.

twelve
The Personal Becomes Political

THE YEAR STARTED OUT PLEASANTLY WITH A MILD adventure.

Ever restless and slow to wear off our wanderlust, in 1987 Snaige made a deal with her brother to take a year off and I did the same with Humber College. We chose to live in Barcelona with our son Dainius, where I would study Spanish in the mornings and write in the afternoons, and Snaige would wander the neighbourhoods doing sketches while our boy was in daycare. There, he would become probably the only child in the world to be briefly trilingual in Lithuanian, Spanish, and Catalan.

We hung on to our ties to Paris, where Snaige would have an art show in a gallery by the Seine and I would attend the wedding of my old *Paris Voices* friend, Ken Timmerman. But our days were mostly spent with local friends Enrique and Teresa Zueras and their son, who was the same age as Dainius. We lived high up from the sea on Avenida de la Virgen de Montserrat, not far from the fantastic Gaudí-designed park with its colourful wall mosaics and unlikely ceramic figures, a place that became our local playground. On weekends we might take the train to the seaside resort of Sitges to swim in the ocean.

I was working on the manuscript of my third novel, disheartened by the lack of a book deal thus far but determined to keep writing. Lithuanians were not on our radar except for the Barcelona visit, engineered by my cousin, of the writer and director Jonas Jurašas and his writer wife, Aušra Marija Sluckaitė-Jurašienė. Both had been expelled from Soviet Lithuania for producing "anti-Soviet" plays. They would go on to be inspiring lifelong friends who lived deeply in culture, writing and staging plays in New York and Toronto and, later, Lithuania again.

But we did have one opportunity to visit Lithuania. The Soviet state invited the children of Lithuanian émigré parents to take a month's summer language course in Vilnius. It was a case of mutual exploitation. The Lithuanian Communists would use soft power to demonstrate to us just how benign the current regime was, and we could take advantage of the program since as regular tourists we would have been allowed only five days in the country. I'd had one such harried visit a decade earlier.

This trip to Vilnius in 1987 came toward the sunset of the old Soviet Union, but that was not obvious at the time. Lithuania's Vilnius had all the typical shortages of Soviet cities, anything from coffee to meat to shoes depending on the moment, but we found there were new "co-operatives," non-state-run restaurants, that signalled a mild loosening of the rules.

Mikhail Gorbachev was on television all the time, preaching reform through his so-called *perestroika*, but Snaige's relatives and mine did not really believe anything would change. And neither did we. Our visit was a chance to get to know the aging and traumatized remnants of our parents' relatives and to get the lay of the land before returning to Barcelona and Canada. Snaige had an art show in Vilnius and we made a few friends there who would become critically important to us in the future.

We did not recognize an early tremor in the Soviet structure then, one that came shortly after we got back to Barcelona. Later that summer, the first Lithuanian protest meeting against Soviet occupation was held in Vilnius near the statue of poet Adomas Mickevičius, another Polish writer who wrote about Lithuania. The opening lines of his long poem *Pan Tadeusz* went right to the heart of my parents' generation's feelings: "Lithuania, my country — you are like good health — only those who have lost you know your worth."

This sort of protest would have been impossible a couple of years earlier. It would have been smashed and the organizers rounded up. But having left the scene, I was barely aware of this protest, and it would take a while for me to understand that something unusual was happening in Soviet Lithuania and beyond.

DOMESTIC LIFE DOMINATED MY THOUGHTS. Upon our return to Canada, I switched from teaching ESL to freshman composition, and our second son, Gintaras, was born on May 3, 1988. Coincidentally, a group called *Sajūdis* (The Movement) was formed in Lithuania on the same day. They were thirty-five prominent intellectuals whose intention was to support the perestroika reforms of Gorbachev, since ordinary communist structures in the state were slow to evolve. But this support for reforms was to transform into something very different very quickly.

My enlightenment came late that summer, when a politically savvy Lithuanian neighbour named Al Juzukonis invited me over to watch a video of both the Vilnius protest I had not witnessed and another of which I was unaware.

I couldn't believe my eyes.

I stepped out of his house and onto the street as if awakening from some sort of *Pleasantville* dream. The world I had inhabited was going to crumble and the lives of millions were going to be transformed. It was as if I had seen a secret previously hidden in plain sight.

When I did awake to the seismic events that had begun, I found that most everyone else I knew in Canada,

Lithuanian or not, was still sleeping, as I had been so recently. I had never thought the world I inhabited would change very much, unless by nuclear accident or global warming. Politically, we had been locked into a bipolar world my entire life.

Now I knew that a storm was looming and it was going to have impact far beyond that particular Soviet Socialist Republic. I needed to get involved somehow, to get close to see what was happening. I went on a tear through the Lithuanian community like some sort of Paul Revere, riding hard to warn that the enemy was coming — or more precisely, coming apart.

I pitched an investigative trip to *Saturday Night* magazine, where I knew Anne Collins and subsequently George Galt, and to compensate for not covering travel expenses they gave me two assignments.

I was alive with excitement and burning to get into the story. My bewildered but supportive dean at the college, Pam Hanft, let me take off for a couple of weeks in the middle of the semester once I found a replacement. And poor Snaige, now with an infant as well as a toddler, gave me carte blanche to chase down a once-in-a-lifetime story.

When I landed in Lithuania that October, it was a week after a major Sajūdis meeting, and the streets were alive with small groups talking on streetcorners and bigger ones huddling in parks and squares. There were mini-protests in various places, from a hunger striker camped out by the cathedral to knots of people reading newly posted stories on a kind of democracy wall bulletin board across the street.

Suddenly history was happening right now, and the memories of postwar mass deportations and repressions, squelched armed resistance, and the Catholic underground filled not only the boulevards but also newspapers and handmade news sheets passed about on sidewalks.

Times were electrifying but tumultuous and unstable. When I had a driver take me a few hours north to Šiauliai to meet a group of resistance priests, we were tailed back that night along the highway. The follower in his car played cat and mouse with us — zooming ahead, falling behind and turning on high beams, riding along beside us, and pointing at us through his passenger side window.

"What does this mean?" I asked my driver.

"He's sending a message. They know all about us."

"What do you think they will do?"

"That's anybody's guess. I'm just keeping both hands on the wheel."

That part turned out to be simple intimidation. And the flip side of the intimidation by a mysterious adherent of the old regime was a surprising crack in the new local Communist leadership. My Lithuanian artist friend, Mindaugas Šnipas, managed to get me a meeting with the freshly installed chairman of the Lithuanian Communist Party, Algirdas Brazauskas. The Communists were trying to take control of events by putting in unsullied new faces at the top of the local regime. Brazauskas was just such a character.

Walking into the offices of the Central Committee of the Communist Party of Lithuania was like walking in to visit some sort of mafia don in his lair. The lights in the halls were off but most of the office doors were open, and in those doorways leaned men in suits, one or two of them smoking, eyeing me up and down as I walked along.

Inside the massive office, Algirdas Brazauskas, genial and built like a tractor driver from a propaganda poster, came across as a new style of communist — reasonable, a supporter of Gorbachev. He said the reforms were good, that everything was headed in the right direction as long as hotheads did not take over the reform movement.

But a great unravelling had begun. No new face was going to permit the old structure to survive.

On my flight back home through Moscow, I had a moment of insight about my parents and their generation, as well as mine. I was playing a small role in this upheaval, reporting on it. My parents' generation would have expected me to "do my bit." They had made me and others of my generation into sleeper agents.

All of that Lithuanian community business our parents had put us through — the Saturday schools, the folk dancing, the parish and its various organizations from Boy Scouts to drama groups — had a hidden purpose. We were trained to be soldiers, passive for the moment, but primed to rise up when the day came for Lithuania to seek its independence. And rise up we did, by the thousands. A great many of us in the international diaspora would work to help free Lithuania in any way we could, and my way was through words.

My part of the struggle against the old Soviet Union on my return to Canada was two-pronged. Within the Ontario Lithuanian community, I made the rounds of various local Lithuanian organizations to proclaim that the day of Lithuania's rising was upon us. I felt like Peter reporting what he had seen at Christ's tomb, but I was delivering my message in suburban recreation rooms and parish halls. There were many, many doubting Thomases. I wanted people in the community to donate fax machines to Sajūdis, to buy tape recorders for reform-minded journalists, to speak to their local politicians, above all to act and to act firmly and fast.

I developed credibility when the *Saturday Night* articles came out, and then came the second prong. Outside the community, I became "Mr. Lithuania" to the Canadian media. Harry Philips and Daniel Schwartz at CBC Television's *The National* asked for briefings, and I wrote about Lithuania for *The Globe and Mail* and *Toronto Star*. I sat in on radio and television shows explaining things I had learned in Saturday school but that no one had ever heard about in Canada. "Where was Lithuania?" On the Baltic Sea, across from Sweden. "Had it ever existed as a state?" Yes, both before World War Two and well before that, as the biggest nation in Europe in the fifteenth century. "Were the Lithuanians a type of Russian or Slav?" No — Baltic people, a separate, non-Slavic group.

A couple of ambivalences in the general public came up, not significant to me at the time but important later. I was talking on a radio call-in show on the subject of Lithuania and the unstable Soviet Union, and a caller wanted to know if the author of the historic Lithuanian national anthem had really been an anti-Semite. I didn't know. I later found out the answer was yes. I heard about a cautious newspaper article in the American press wondering if the Lithuanians should be permitted to seek self-government given their history in the war — namely, their participation in the Holocaust.

And then, as the story of a crumbling Soviet Union and the Lithuanian part within it became more widely known, other sorts of questions came up, often from friends. "Shouldn't Lithuanians be content with a liberalized Soviet Union?" No. They had been independent between 1917 and 1940 and wanted to be independent again. "We can understand the freedom of East Germany and Poland after the collapse of the Berlin Wall, but shouldn't the borders of the USSR be respected?" No. Those colonial borders were achieved by relatively recent Soviet conquest and must be torn down.

As I became radicalized, people anxious about broader unrest in the world asked me to calm down and make the Lithuanians in Lithuania calm down too, because the actions of those hotheads threatened the peace of Canadians.

I was having dinner in the beautiful loft apartment of the writers Margaret Cannon and John Bentley Mays when John brought up that argument again. I was too irritated by that time to take it sitting down. I half rose from my place over the dinner table littered with baguette crusts and cheese rinds and leaned over with hands braced against the table. I responded that my peace-loving friend John Mays and his squash-playing pals were irrelevant to people fighting for their freedom. Not just irrelevant, but despicably self-centred.

It's the kind of thing you can only say to a friend. I'm not even sure if John ever played squash.

By now, everyone had woken up. My generation of Lithuanians was mobilized and doing all it could around the world to put pressure on our governments to support the Lithuanians, and of course Estonians, Latvians, and others, in the struggle to break away from the Soviet

Union. Our government was supportive, but with limits, fearing to push too hard.

In a feverish pitch, I kept my passport with me at all times, in case I ever needed to travel abroad at short notice. As events unfolded, Lithuanians moved from reform to explicit plans to declare independence, notwithstanding the opposition of Gorbachev and the Kremlin — to say nothing of the opposition of reluctant Western powers that wished Lithuanians and others like them would do Gorbachev a favour by staying obediently within the USSR.

I travelled to Lithuania for radio and magazines a few times and upon return was consumed by the unfolding Soviet story even in Canada. To the surprise of my fellow faculty in a shared office at Humber College, I'd get as many as a dozen calls a day from Lithuanian colleagues bringing news of the latest developments or from magazines wanting information. Once there was even a query about how to get arms into Lithuania if the need arose.

Came the hour, came the people.

None of us had experience in trying to make a captive country like Lithuania independent. Who could have known and how could one have prepared? In one publication, I called this activity by the Lithuanian refugees and their children "the church basement against the Kremlin," because those of us with Lithuanian heritage all knew one another from those parochial basements and from our childhoods. None of us was an expert in what we were trying to do.

Some were raising money for an emergency ship-to-shore telephone system, in case the Lithuanian Parliament was closed down. In the days before social media, our "grandmother network" was fast and thorough in communicating actions to be taken. Three grandmothers could hit the phones and we could have several hundred demonstrators out in Nathan Phillips Square in Toronto by the next day. I worked with a tight group trying to keep the distracted media and the cautious and nervous federal government onside.

ON THE AFTERNOON of March 11, 1990, I stood with hundreds of others in the Lithuanian House on Toronto's Bloor Street to listen to a direct radio feed of the vote from the Lithuanian Chamber of Deputies.

Things had evolved so far in Lithuania that a newly elected group of supposedly Soviet delegates was planning to put an end to the Soviet part of Lithuania and formally declare independence. It seemed so impossible, like something from our parents' fantasies, ones that we'd so often dismissed.

And in that hall in Toronto, on a chalkboard, my brother Joe kept tally of the votes as they came in one by one, as described by a dispassionate voice in Lithuania:

"In favour of independence. Next vote. The vote is aye."

"In favour of independence. Next vote. The vote is aye."

And so on as the number of ayes rose with only an occasional abstention.

A CHEER WENT UP in our hall on Bloor Street when the impossible happened on the far side of the Baltic Sea as a vast majority voted to break away from the Soviet Union. We were euphoric. Many of us wept because we never thought we would see the day and a dozen of us poured into a fancy local restaurant called the Villa Borghese to celebrate. My exuberant friend, the lawyer Al Pace, felt a need to wander to other tables and explain to strangers the reason for our celebration.

We were overwhelmed with emotion, and I needed to seek a reference for it. I was trained in English, and all my references were English, so I thought of the St. Crispin's Day speech from Shakespeare's *Henry V*, in which Henry talks about how the battle of Agincourt will be remembered by those few who were going on to fight so many, and how they will show their battle scars on each anniversary.

We lucky ones in Canada had no wounds to show, no scars to reveal if we rolled up sleeves. But achieving independence wasn't as simple as declaring it. Within a year, in January of 1991, fourteen Lithuanian civilians died during an attack at the Vilnius television tower and hundreds more were wounded one night during a death spasm of the tyrannical old Soviet regime. The survivors of those clashes would be the ones with the real scars.

The day after that attack, my phone rang again and again with news organizations wondering what the Lithuanians would do next.

The answer: people in Vilnius quickly came out onto the streets to protect the Parliament Buildings.

I was in the CBC TV newsroom for producer Daniel Schwartz, trying to get a line into the Parliament. I finally reached Ramūnas Bogdanas, advisor to independence leader Vytautas Landsbergis, and Bogdanas told television host Barbara Frum that he expected he would die under an anticipated Soviet attack on the Parliament Buildings. Lithuanian parliamentarians took mass confession and benediction in expectation of being slaughtered. Volunteers on the rooftop of the Parliament assembled Molotov cocktails in preparation for the defence.

In 1940, Lithuania had bowed to an ultimatum by the Soviets and lost independence without a fight. For decades after that, the county had to live under the lie that it had voluntarily joined the Soviet Union. That was not going to happen this time. This time the Lithuanians would resist.

I also managed to reach a fellow Canadian in Vilnius, Tom Zizys, who had a view of the Lithuanian Parliament

Buildings from an apartment across the street. Inside those buildings was another Torontonian, Mirga Saltmiras, who had let her father know that sometimes people had to die for their principles and she might be one of them.

The Lithuanians could have been crushed like the Hungarians in 1956 or the Czechoslovaks in 1968. Martial law could have come down in Lithuania as it did in Poland in 1981. Within the country, groups of quislings were preparing to step up once Moscow regained control.

Then the immediate pressure inexplicably eased. The attack on the television tower may have been an attempt by Gorbachev to assert dominance, but repression would have needed to be cranked up, and the man may have lost the nerve to keep on killing. In any case, the larger drama was now being played out in Moscow, where a putsch by old-school Soviet hardliners was attempted and failed.

Lithuania's fight for independence finally came to fruition during the general collapse of the Soviet Union eight months later. I was at a remote northern cottage in August of 1991 when it happened. My neighbour, Keith Stokes, came by to tell me the Soviet Union was over. I left my holidaying family behind and went by boat and car to the village of Bala, and from a pay phone there found out from my Lithuanian friends in Toronto that it was true.

In that phone booth in an Ontario summer resort town, I found out the dream of independence had been achieved. The Canadian government was flying then finance minister Michael Wilson for formal recognition ceremonies and invited me along as an interpreter.

But I couldn't go. I'd taken so much time off my college teaching that I was borderline AWOL. I had to stay behind to teach grammar to college kids. My older brother Andy stepped up to take on that role.

Besides, for me, now it was time for other things.

thirteen
Turning Away, Turning Back

MY PHONE CEASED RINGING. NOBODY NEEDED NEWS OF Lithuania anymore. All was quiet on this side of the Atlantic as the Lithuanians went about building their newly independent nation. I wanted for a time to go there with my family and join them, but Snaige was against it. She said our parents were old and would soon need help. She owned a business with her brother and the children were doing well in school.

I was thirty-eight at the time, and the opportunity to go there belonged to a generation about a decade younger, many of whom did go to live, or try to live, in developing Lithuania. Had those of us in the struggle been soldiers, we would have been demobilized. We were not soldiers, but it was still time to return to our regular lives. That first year was very hard because I did not know what to do with myself. I was in a post-revolutionary miasma. Now what?

THE BOYS WERE STILL YOUNG and needed care. My work at the college was consuming in a good way, and I was learning how to build up at the cottage: a cabin here, a shed there. A lot of chopping wood for the stove. I perfected baking skills. All very calm. Slightly dull, though.

Slowly I returned to fiction, but it was not easy. Fiction has no deadline. No one calls late in the evening wanting an update. For the most part, no one was interested at all. But I kept at my craft and sullen art and finally published a first novel in 1994. I was forty-one years old then and was asked what took me so long to publish. I'd been busy, I said.

That novel was called *Dinner at the End of the World*, a sardonic take on global warming. It had good reviews, but not many took notice. I did better with a book of linked stories that came out three years later called *Buying on Time*. That book was mostly humour about a family of immigrants adapting to life in Canada from the 1950s to the 1980s. It was nominated for a Leacock Medal for Humour as well as a Toronto Book Award and was serialized on radio. Later, it would go on to be translated into Italian, Chinese, and Lithuanian.

I was so tired of Lithuanians that I made no mention of the family's ethnic origins in that book. They were just generic Eastern Europeans, because I wanted to represent a broader immigrant experience. But my editor, John Metcalf, insisted that I identify them, so I reluctantly threw in a wry mention of the family's nationality in a few throwaway lines at the end of the book, set in the 1980s before the collapse of the Soviet Union. Here they are:

> "You know what I hate about the name of the homeland?" Gerry finally asked.
> "What?"
> "The name."
> "It's just a name," I said.
> "Yeah, but it sounds corny."
> I said it out loud. "Lithuania."
> "Gerry's right," said Tom. "It's embarrassing. And nobody knows where it is. It's one of those nonexistent countries."
> "And it's going to stay that way," said Gerry. "The Iron Curtain is going to last another hundred years. Even the sound of the name bugs me. It's the ending. All the funny countries have funny endings on them. Bulgaria, Albania, Estonia, Lusitania."
> "The last one was a ship," I said.
> "But it was named after a Roman province," Tom said. "Gerry means it sounds like we're from some kind of comic opera. Like we're from Ruritania."

AT THAT TIME, around 1997, my mother inadvertently tipped me in a direction that I would follow for the rest of my literary life.

Her generation, the immigrants from Lithuania to Canada, was dying out. She herself would pass away two years later. And as her cohort went, mine, their children, cleaned up the old houses and cleared out the old be-longings left behind.

What to do with that generation's Lithuanian books? My generation, with few exceptions, did not read Lithuanian books. We found the memoirs trod an immigration path we'd heard about too often; the actual classics of Lithuanian literature were remote from our lives; and the literature written under the Soviet regime felt distant as well. By that point, in my mid-forties, I had read many Lithuanian newspapers and magazines, but I must have read fewer than half a dozen Lithuanian books.

I found it hard to read Lithuanian literature and if I had to rate my language skills at the time, I'd say I'd almost achieved the level of a bright semi-literate Lith-uanian peasant, but with serious vocabulary short-comings. I was without any knowledge of the names of birds, trees, flowers, farm implements, automobile parts, or sexual organs. The latter in particular. Our parents' was a modest generation.

We were at her Wasaga cottage when my mother pre-sented me with a Lithuanian memoir she had picked up in the parish basement hall for a quarter. It came from one of the immigrant collections of books no one knew what to do with.

This particular Lithuanian memoir was on subject matter I had never read before. It was an autobiography by Lithuania's prominent interwar sculptor Petras Rimša. He wrote about his rural nineteenth-century background and then his education in art, first in Poland and later in Paris, at about the same time as the slightly younger Jewish sculptor, also from Lithuania, Jacques Lipchitz.

The story of this raw boy being taught how to behave among the gentry in Poland was very touching. Even more touching were stories of his early days as a student in Paris, and his nervousness in his first life drawing class.

"'Have you ever seen a naked woman before?' my teacher asked me as the model was about to disrobe.

"'Once by accident,' I replied shyly, 'and I looked away.'"

And yet people like the shy Rimša and provincial Lipchitz went on to become important makers of modern art. Lipchitz was the first cubist sculptor. I began to do a little reading about artists in Paris. I discovered that Constantin Brâncuși, the man who first made abstract sculpture in Europe, came from Romanian peasant stock. Yet another cutting-edge modernist had rural roots.

My mind caught fire. I was now animated in a literary way that was similar to the excitement I had felt during Lithuania's reach for independence. I talked about modernity with my friend, the art critic John Bentley Mays. I wondered why "modern" art was developed by "primitives" and he rambled into the story of Josephine

Baker, who played the "primitive" with irony and great success at the Folies Bergère in Paris. When the poet e. e. cummings saw Baker dance for the first time, he claimed she heralded the arrival of modern times.

I began to see the periphery of Europe, those "backward" places, as sources of the cutting-edge modern. Even "provincial" America had produced Baker. And what made certain provincials arriving in Paris famous and others not? And what was fame anyway — a roll of fate's dice or a justified laurel for talent? I leaned toward the former interpretation.

I was strongly influenced by the story of three young artist friends who studied at the Vilnius Art Academy and travelled to Paris together before the First World War. There they struggled together until one of them, Chaïm Soutine, had sixty of his works bought in one day by the American collector Albert Barnes. We remember Soutine, but we have more or less forgotten his former friends, Pinchus Krémègne and Michel Kikoïne. In their youth, their work had seemed similar, but luck smiled on Soutine while the other two lived on to embittered old age.

These artists came from "the periphery." A book reviewer would later remark that a novel of mine set in Lithuania described actions at "the periphery." I mulled over this stinging comment. It revealed the reviewer's colonial mindset by positing that centres such as New

York (but not all of New York — just Manhattan, and maybe Brooklyn), London, and Paris were the only places where things mattered. Everywhere else was peripheral, by definition provincial. By this measure, Canada was peripheral as well, because for all the contributions Canada has made worldwide, we are still marginal to major events.

This idea of the periphery revealed a hierarchical mindset, as if significance and history were determined by a colonial world view.

I HAD DETERMINED in my youth that I could not be English and so ultimately killed Tony to become Antanas. I was now turning away from Canadian subject matter to set all of my fiction in Europe, primarily Lithuania. But my audience was going to be Canadian, or anyway English speakers.

Why Lithuania? Because so many dramatic things happened there, on that small stage. The struggles there reveal not some sort of distant heartache *on the periphery*. They reveal the human heart and how it reacts under extreme pressure in one of the places in the world where the worst things happened, a territory historian Timothy Snyder included in *Bloodlands*. It was perhaps the worst of places for Jews in the Holocaust.

I had the language, which gave me access to a world outside my everyday one. I dove into a parallel world much different from Canada but peopled with humans like everywhere else.

Not only was Lithuania a small place where big things happened, it was also far enough away from me that I could focus on it properly. It was as if I was far-sighted in literary terms. I could not focus on anything that was too close. I needed to put some distance between myself and my subject matter.

I had been raised in Canada with insistence on my heritage. I turned away from the parts of ethnic life that I found banal. But I discovered there were stories in Lithuania that I could mine for their dramatic resonance. And the more I did research there, among old books and archives and by walking the streets, the more I found.

This approach to my material could even be considered a form of literary exile. Some writers needed to leave their countries before they could write about them. I was "exiled" from Lithuania in literary terms. I didn't leave the place because I was never there, and it took on all the mythical qualities of absent places.

I wrote about Lithuania and artists in Paris in a novel called *Woman in Bronze*. By then, I had fallen so deeply into reading about Lithuania in the twentieth century that Lithuanian friends of mine would telephone after their parents had died so I could go through their left-over libraries. I'd pluck out obscure memoirs and histories about village life, imprisonment in the Stutthof concentration camp, deportation to the gulag, killings of Jews at various execution pits, collectivization, and postwar resistance to the Soviets.

I chose the latter as the subject of another novel I called *Underground*. We live so deeply in the West here that for us the war ended in May of 1945, but all through parts of Eastern Europe, the Soviets returned to the places they had first terrorized and turned life into a different kind of hell from the hell of German occupation. And for different groups. If on the one hand the Jews were the primary victims of the Germans, on the other hand farm and business owners, policemen, and former mid-level government bureaucrats were the new victims under the Soviets.

Today I read sometimes about fading knowledge of the Holocaust among young people in the West. But if fewer and fewer know about that monstrosity, next to nobody remembers the gulag except for a generation that was around when Solzhenitsyn popularized the word. And even among that cohort, the gulag seems to have become slightly boring, and reference to it is seen as a sign of conservatism.

In 2005, Snaige was asked by the Canadian Embassy Office to put on an art exhibition in Vilnius, where we had not been for thirteen years. The call came through Darius Ross, one of a younger generation of Canadians with Lithuanian heritage who had gone over to live there. We thought it was also going to be a chance for our boys, Dainius at twenty-one and Gintaras at seventeen, to see some of their heritage and meet some of their distant cousins. My sons had the language, so they could communicate as much or as little as they chose. I would go along as the family driver.

At the time, I was again writing fiction set in Lithuania but had lost touch with its modern reality. The place had changed a lot since I'd last seen it. In Vilnius, a whole gang of high-rise glass office buildings now stood on the far side of the Neris River where the city planners had banished them, so as to be outside the medieval city centre. But they glowered there, tall and intimidating, from across the water.

The Lithuania I remembered from previous visits was post-Soviet, but this was a place with full supermarkets and tourist groups being led through the city by guides speaking Italian, Spanish, and German. Our boys were drinking it in and Snaige was wrapped up in preparations for her show. Darius thought I might be an interesting interview subject for an hour-long television interview show run by an intellectual named Leonidas Donskis. This brilliant philosopher did not do fluff — he asked complicated, three-part questions, some of which were so abstract I could barely follow them, but I answered as best I could. Then Dalia Kuizinienė, a literature teacher, asked me to speak to some of her students.

One thing led to another. I had been found again by the Lithuanians, in the way Snaige and I had been found in Paris. Leonidas Donskis and his wife Jolanta belonged to the group that had carried on the tradition of the pre-independence conferences. I was invited to speak in one such program and Lithuanian publisher Versus Aureus asked to translate and publish *Woman in Bronze*.

In my youth I was used to searching for Lithuania in various places, including the library stacks, and now Lithuania was looking for me, in particular after *Underground* was published there in translation. The novel was based on memoirs of Lithuanian postwar anti-Soviet partisans and I was invited to present it at the Vilnius Book Fair.

I was a novelty in Lithuania, first because I wrote about the place in English and second because not much had been written in fiction to that point on the subject of the postwar anti-Soviet resistance. Patriots believed it to be the untold history whereas a minority insisted on the criminality of the so-called "forest brothers." I used my research of the most well-known partisan to write a novel that I hoped showed some complexity in human psychology, rather than painting the fighters as simple heroes or villains.

I was unprepared for the level of interest when I arrived on a February weekend in 2012 for the annual

Vilnius Book Fair — I ended up with back-to-back inter-
views on television, radio, and in print, so much so there
was no time to eat between each event. The book fair itself was astonishing to me. Over sixty thousand people
showed up over four days to listen to multiple speakers
in multiple halls each hour and to buy discounted books.
The hall where I gave my talk on *Underground* must have
had room for three hundred. Not only were all the seats
taken, the crowd standing at the door was many layers
thick.

I had stumbled into a book culture unlike anything
I had ever seen in Canada. The taxi driver who took me
to the event wanted to discuss electronic books versus
paper books. The publishers' counters were swarmed by
buyers looking for deals. It was like being at a nightclub
where the bartenders were so busy you needed to be
beautiful or insistent to catch their attention.

I fell into a controversy about that novel because I'd
used the outline of the life of the most famous partisan
of them all, Juozas Lukša, who had fought the Soviets,
escaped to France where he married, and then returned
on a doomed CIA mission to continue the fight in the
1950s. His widow hated the idea that I'd taken his
story and fictionalized it, and her displeasure ran in
newspapers all across the country.

I didn't mind. She had a right to her opinions, and I
had a right to create novels.

Lithuania continued to find me after I'd already published a few novels in English, and the frequent catch-up translation of my work made me appear in more rapid succession there than I did in Canada, where it sometimes took seven years for me to finish a book and be published. And since book culture was so strong in Lithuania, the novels were covered on television, especially when I won the Book of the Year prize there in 2018 for my memoir, *The Barefoot Bingo Caller*.

The ceremony took place in one of the big halls at the Vilnius Book Fair with flowers and speeches and in the presence of the Minister of Culture. Because of the literary prize, the book was promoted all over national television night after night after night.

THE "BACK AND FORTHNESS" of immigrants and the children of immigrants makes for halls of mirrors. I write about Lithuania in English and then have that book translated into Lithuanian and have to explain to Lithuanians how I depict that country to Canadians. Here in English Canada, I am in a niche that is not really a niche, because immigrant literature by writers such as David Chariandy, Andrew Borkowski, Kim Thúy, and many others makes up such a large part of what is published here.

Lithuania is a small country and the old city of Vilnius has a compact but charming centre. Sooner or later, if you know people in Vilnius, you will run across them in that centre, along with celebrities you see regularly on television or politicians from the Parliament Buildings up the road. After I had appeared a great deal on television, I began to be recognized on the street, and once my waitress, a literature student studying my work, wanted a photograph.

Lithuanians are often modest, and I have been asked if I am satisfied with my literary reception there and how it compares to my literary reputation in Canada. I have done well enough in Canada, but we are Canadians — so first of all, our emotions are more muted, and secondly, though literary events do happen here, they tend not to happen on television unless it has to do with the Giller Prize.

A friend once sent me a photo of a student on the Toronto subway reading one of my books. That's what I call Canadian celebrity. I am grateful for it. We don't have book reviews and art reviews on national TV every night, and the odds of anyone except Margaret Atwood and a few others being recognized on the street are pretty small.

That's OK. I write about there for here, and now here has been translated there, and it is bewildering and wonderful.

And to my astonishment, the Italians and the Chinese have also translated some of my work, so somewhere in Asia there is a reader finding out what it was like to be a Lithuanian immigrant to Canada in the 1950s or an aspiring Lithuanian artist in Paris in the 1920s.

There is no end to my scribbling. At this writing I have just released a new novel, called *Some Unfinished Business*, set where else but there? And another novel is in the works. I'm getting old faster than I'm running out of subject matter. I need to rush to write up my latest dreams.

fourteen
Professor Sileika in the Literary Trenches

IN THE 1990S, SPRAWLING HUMBER COLLEGE NORTH was a massive conglomeration of architectural ideas mashed together in a suburban industrial wasteland near Toronto's Pearson airport. More than a training school and less than a university, it was the place young people went to learn to be chemistry technicians, chefs, architectural designers, and above all generic "businesspeople." And all of them needed to take a couple of composition classes.

This was where many aspiring English PhD grads landed when the university academic market dried up in the 1980s and '90s. Study of Keats and Shelley, attendance at literary readings by Irving Layton and Margaret Atwood, and weekends spent following the literary news in magazines and newspapers all led to teaching sleepy chemistry students how to write five-paragraph essays at eight o'clock on a Monday morning. It could have been worse. The hospitality kids had been cooking since seven in the morning, and their shot at the essay came from three to five in the afternoon.

There were no "English" teachers. The old-fashioned word had been banished in case anyone thought we were teaching anything as impractical as poetry. Colleges were all about practical achievements. We were "communications" teachers. Not even "teachers." Initially we were called "masters," but the word became problematic. Two problems were solved when the union demanded we be called "professors." It got rid of the unfortunate old term and elevated us with an honorific which ordinarily took a university lecturer many years to achieve.

The title was useful on credit card applications, health forms, and with unaware neighbours. Real university professors tended to look at us sardonically.

If there were many stymied academics in our ranks, I was not one of them. I'd worked my way into freshman composition by following the trail of ESL graduates who were trying to retrain in the education system and found it hard to pass communications courses designed for native speakers. I became involved in redesigning their communications program while being tut-tutted by conservative colleagues concerned about dropping standards.

And all I ever had was a BA in English, somewhat below the standard the colleges wanted their teachers to have. But I was interested and involved, and the administration, including Pam Hanft, the tough but supportive dean, let me help create new courses.

Literature and Lithuania and family and friends were my main concerns, but I spent most of my working days in the college. Conversation with the other communications teachers was good, and at the big faculty lunch tables, I might end up with the HVAC crew, the funeral directors, or the accountants, and this exposure took me out of my English silo.

One of the downsides of teaching freshman composition was the marking load. A garage mechanic once laughingly told me that as a teacher, I was already semi-retired, but marking up to a thousand papers each semester required extreme focus and time management. How well I remember Thanksgiving weekends, which fell just before the date when mid-terms were due. Drinks during the day were out of the question, and every short walk or drive to look at the fall colours was paid for by the number of papers I marked first: five papers for a walk if it was short, ten or fifteen for a drive because who knew, we might stop somewhere to buy apples and the minutes until mid-term marks were due were ticking away.

Little by little, I moved from teaching a humanities survey course to a short stories course to a "world stories" course. I hit the first jackpot in the 1990s when one of my colleagues, Joe Kertes, started a creative writing program and left one department for another to run it. He handed off to me three sections of journalism students who were motivated to learn about grammar and composition. Teaching was easier with them because they were going to make a living with words, unlike, say, the landscaping students, who could envision no life that would ever require an essay.

I'd met Joe back in the 1980s when we'd both been hired full-time. We were about the same age and had European roots and we could lose a whole afternoon talking about writers and writing if the opportunity presented itself, as it often did when we found ourselves smoking together just outside various college doorways. There were a lot of us aspiring writers among the English crew, but he was the first to publish, winning the Leacock Medal for Humour with his novel *Winter Tulips* in 1989.

Eventually Wayson Choy and I joined him in publishing our novels. Michael Helm was there as well, although Michael was a little younger and moved in a different crowd. Joe and Wayson and I would go on to dine regularly for years in order to talk about our successes and failures in writing, and to gossip thoroughly about the people in that pursuit. Wayson was always interested in the "juicy bits." Each of us was writing out of our "ethnic" backgrounds — Joe's was Hungarian Jewish and Wayson's was Chinese Canadian, with stories of Vancouver's Chinese diaspora.

I'd given up work in the literary journal *Descant*, but

went on to talk about books occasionally on radio and television and to review books in newspapers and magazines. Producer Vac Verikaitis at OMNI Television tried to get me to leave teaching to host a television show, but he wanted it to be about immigrants and I really only wanted to talk about books. I guest hosted a bit for CBC Radio's *The Arts Tonight* and briefly shared an interviewing role on TVO's book show *Imprint*, but media were an enjoyable sideline for me. I was primarily a teacher and a writer.

Well into the 1990s, I had found a good life balance. In addition to composition, I was also teaching classes of creative writing — extra work (read: extra income for a stretched budget) from Joe Kertes as he managed both a distance creative writing program and a summer workshop.

I was busy, but managed to keep on writing by compartmentalizing my teaching, my friends, my family, and my literary life. I imagined things could not be better. I wanted nothing to change. Then, in 2002, Joe came to me with an offer I could not refuse. He was being promoted to dean and he needed someone to run the writing program he had created nine years earlier. I was leery of administrative work because I'd seen others fall into the rabbit hole of college admin and have it eat up their entire lives.

"What would I have to do?" I asked.

"You'll buy certain books and find the best, most exciting writers, and then you'll get them to teach for you."

"That's it?"

"That's it."

I was sold.

Joe was ahead of the curve in founding a creative writing program in Canada, which had few at the time. Joe designed both a distance program and summer workshop that brought in the most celebrated Canadian and international writers and made our bedraggled campus up by the airport into a hotbed of literary excitement. Margaret Atwood, Mordecai Richler, Nino Ricci, and Anne Michaels were among the noted Canadian participants, and Richard Ford and D.M. Thomas were among the international luminaries.

Then we moved down to the Lakeshore campus, partly a former psychiatric hospital with beautiful, if melancholy, red-brick buildings around a quad. Unlike the proletarian North Campus, this place looked like an Ivy League school.

That first summer, Joe had me go out to dinner along with the American writer Tim O'Brien, whose work I had often taught, usually the short story collection *The Things They Carried*. O'Brien is a very great talent. I was star-struck and could barely speak over the dinner at the tiny La Palette on Augusta Street in Kensington Market.

They both smiled at my fumbling conversation, but I didn't fumble for long. I was getting to meet one exquisite writer after another.

So began fifteen years where I had one of the best seats in the Canadian English language literary house. We had excellent regular faculty, including writers such as Kim Moritsugu, Olive Senior, John Metcalf, Isabel Huggan, Nino Ricci, Guy Vanderhaeghe, Esi Edugyan, and many more, but international celebrities of the time such as the late Andrea Levy captured the imagination of students and the press.

I hadn't even known who Alistair MacLeod was until one day over coffee in the early 2000s, when broadcaster Shelagh Rogers reached up to her bookshelf where she kept copies of his works to give away. Like many others, I was smitten. I wrote to him, left phone messages, and finally drove up to York University where I heard he was reading and cornered him afterward to get a commitment. He agreed to teach for me, and so he did every summer for another dozen years. I always asked him to close our summer workshop by reading his short story "As Birds Bring Forth the Sun," and this moving piece invariably had an auditorium of students rising in a standing ovation that often included their tears.

Over the years, I managed to hire other prominent writers, such as Miriam Toews, whom I had to force to lunch because she was giving all of her time to her students. Joe and I reached out to David Bezmozgis right after we saw his first published story in *Harper's*. One summer, we managed to host Martin Amis, David Mitchell, and Rachel Kushner, and made enough of a splash to be the subject of an article in *Hello!* magazine. Another year, Joe snagged Edward Albee and the American consulate had us all over to celebrate. Once, a Toronto Star headline read "Humber Dominates Giller List." We had many wonderful teachers, but we live in a celebrity culture, so the best-known ones attracted media and students.

I took it upon myself to attend all the book launches of teachers and many graduates. Among the latter were Dr. Vincent Lam, Shari Lapena, and Cathy Marie Buchanan, to name only a few of the hundreds who published. This meant I sometimes went out to a book launch four out of five nights a week in the spring or the fall, as well as many awards ceremonies, from the Writers' Trust to the Trillium. Alumnus Kenneth Bonert once said to me sardonically, "You've become quite the man about literary town."

And I had. One night I made it home by nine in the evening after briefly making an appearance at three book launches. Another night, I was at home getting ready to leave when Snaige asked me where I was headed. I told her it was another book launch and she said I looked like hell, I looked exhausted, and I was going nowhere.

In case this gives the impression of a literary high life for writers in Canada, I want to add a corrective. Many writers in Canada have some of the worst financial lives I know of in the class of well-educated people. Positions like mine were rare, and those writers without good day jobs or supportive spouses barely scraped by. *Quill and Quire*, the industry monthly magazine, featured a writer on each cover. If you ever appeared on the cover, which should have been a sign of success, odds were one-in-ten that you'd be begging me for work at Humber within the year.

I regularly had one or two requests for work from writers each week, and some of them were desperate. I also sat on the Woodcock committee of the Writers' Trust at the time. This is an organization that hands out unadvertised grants of a few thousand dollars to writers in extreme financial distress. The fund was intended to help writers get over a temporary hump, but many, many of the applicants had problems that were far from temporary.

One applicant had quit an academic position to move to the countryside where life was cheaper in order to devote himself to his novels and subsist until he made a decent income from his writing. Over the years, the family had sunk more and more deeply into poverty. His wife and children were part of the shipwreck of his career in letters.

So many graduates of creative writing programs dream of literary success paired with financial success, but that almost never happens. Others imagine teaching creative writing will help to keep them in a related enterprise, but the teaching field is intensely competitive. The best way of getting a creative writing teaching position is by being a successful and acknowledged writer, but how can one survive long enough to get there?

Success in the arts has always been hard, and writing is no exception. The one place where I have seen many young successful writers is in a shared space with film and television writers. There I saw people making a living at what they did, but I don't know enough about the field to say what their success rate might be.

So many good writers came through in my fifteen years at Humber, and so many students went on to publish, but by 2017 I had been at it long enough. Joe and half the staff I worked with were retiring. It was time to move on. I had two books coming, one just before and one just after retirement. They were a comic memoir called *The Barefoot Bingo Caller* and a genre espionage piece set in Lithuania in 1921 called *Provisionally Yours*, which would be turned into both a Lithuanian feature film and TV serial in 2023.

I had plans for two others, *Some Unfinished Business*, which would come out in 2023, and *The Seaside Café Metropolis*, as yet unpublished at this writing. And then

Stonehewer Books contracted me to write the words you are now reading.

So there was no departing from the literary life when I left the Humber School for Writers in the competent hands of David Bezmozgis and Alissa York. I was just moving on to another phase.

fifteen
New Roots

My Lithuania lay mostly in books. I read Lithuanian histories, memoirs, and novels to find the settings and historical events that I would use in my own writing. Such a small place, and so much drama happened there! That was the Lithuania of my mind, a kind of imaginary Lithuania, not because the place did not exist but because it was the place of my fiction. At times I thought of it as the perfect distance away from me in space and time.

I visited the country to listen to lectures and promote my translations, but I didn't have friends of my childhood or youth there. I had few remaining cousins. Snaige's relatives were closer both in blood and to Vilnius, but I didn't see them that often. I visited post-independence Lithuania for research purposes but also, beyond that, for inexplicable reasons of attraction. It was a parallel world.

My sons, for their part, showed greater or lesser interest in the place. One eventually decided to make his life there.

But the contrast between the worlds I inhabit consists not only of proximate Canada and distant Lithuania, but also larger Canada and "Little Lithuania" right here in Toronto. I'm lucky enough to have a community among the Lithuanians with whom I grew up. The diaspora Lithuanians of my generation were neither just Canada nor just Lithuania, but yet another parallel world that I inhabited from time to time, through a portal to our shared past. Over the decades, mostly we just saw each other at parish weddings and funerals and Christmas and Easter. Small though this world was, it remained dear to me. It consisted of the small town I had grown up in and never really left, despite escape attempts.

My diaspora community shared memories in a way similar to the family history I shared with my two brothers. With Andy and Joe, especially now at a later age, we can spend multiple evenings chewing over what happened to the family in the past and speculating on the unknowable unrecorded facts of our parents' lives during the war and earlier. With my childhood friends of Lithuanian heritage, I have sat in an ice-fishing hut parsing the lives of all the kids like us with whom we grew up.

And if this in any way sounds parochial, I alert the dismissive reader to William Faulkner's *Absalom, Absalom!*, in which two men do exactly that. We who were boys at summer camp can replay the shenanigans of our youth as coloured by the immigrant lives of our parents, all striving to succeed here or wallowing in melancholy for their losses.

Snaige, for her part, has for decades been painting, drawing, and travelling Canada annually with a group of artists. Her friendships in Toronto are deep and long-lasting, going as far back as elementary school. Despite a big retrospective art show she had in Vilnius, our base would continue to be in Toronto.

Thus we live here, and not there, but so much of my belief system was formed by there, not by here.

IN MY NOVELS, the characters often suffer from diminished agency because they tread a much narrower path than is permitted in most western novels. The forces of history bear down on my characters, limiting their options. One reader asked me why so many of my novels ended tragically, and I said I was describing events in Eastern Europe, a place where happy endings seem to reside primarily in imported Disney movies.

As in fiction, so in life. History bore down on Eastern Europe after the invasion and annexation of Ukrainian Crimea by Russia in 2014.

During the time of raised tensions after the invasion, when it seemed Russia might go for Lithuania too, the government published a civil defense book that reminded each Lithuanian that he or she was obliged to defend the country with any weapon possible, all the way down to throwing a stone. It gave instructions on how to tape windows so shards did not fly from nearby explosions.

The booklet pictured Russian tanks and weapons so citizens could recognize them and alert the government of what arms were being used to invade the neighbourhood.

I became alarmed. At the time, I told Snaige that if an invasion came to Lithuania, I'd find a way to put myself there to record what I saw. I had read the diary of Petras Klimas, a prominent writer who had stayed in Vilnius during the German occupation of World War One. His was virtually the only record of day-to-day local events at that time, and I thought it might be a role for me if history repeated itself. What I didn't take account of at the time, something we learned about during the subsequent war in Ukraine, was that Russian occupying forces did not let suspect civilian actions go unpunished.

I alerted my son who lived there that if the invasion came, troops would pour in from south, north, and east, and the only way to get out would be across the Baltic to Sweden. This was a strange conversation. I had never imagined that I would ever be having words like this with him. It felt like the sort of conversation my parents had with their relatives toward the end of the Second World War.

The moment of panic in 2014 seemed to pass. For us in the West, it began to seem as if Crimea's occupation was one of those regional conflicts without wider implications.

At about the same time, I was asked to sit on an advisory committee to the Lithuanian Parliament. There were ten delegates from around the world who joined ten parliamentarians from various parties. I would be the one from Canada to go over twice a year to discuss with the government the needs of the diaspora, of whom there were hundreds of thousands, and the needs of Lithuania that these émigrés might help meet.

My heightened sensitivity to all things Lithuanian made me feel like a Cassandra in Canada. The Baltic States are very far away, and many Canadians would have a hard time finding them on a map. I don't blame them. I'd be hard pressed to carefully map out the borders of the countries of the former Yugoslavia.

But Canadian lack of geographic knowledge is often matched by a lack of knowledge of history and of Eastern European politics as well. The place is far away. At a lawn party in Toronto's expensive Rosedale neighbourhood not long after the invasion of Crimea, the hostess, with a glass of Cava in her hand, went on at some length to me about the foolishness of sending Canadian troops to Latvia, to bolster the NATO eastern front against the Russians. As she spoke, I could only think of Neville Chamberlain's words from 1938, in which he described Germany's invasion of Czechoslovakia as "a quarrel in a faraway country between people of whom we know nothing."

I often needed to speak up about the defense of NATO's eastern flank, and not infrequently was met with polite skepticism in response. Indeed, at times I felt again like one of those pitiful Eastern European dreamers in the works of John le Carré.

I have a long-time circle of Canadian friends who good-naturedly consider me something of a "typical" Eastern European, a little abrupt in general and hawkish about the Russian threat. It is as if all Eastern Europeans are somewhat ridiculous. A kind of *Borat*-syndrome pall continues to hover over all things Eastern European for many people in North America.

For most of my acquaintances over here, the concerns of the Eastern Europeans seemed exaggerated. When I'd talk about Crimea, friends might dismiss my concerns and even raise gentle support for the Russians, saying the people in Ukraine speak Russian — implying, as Putin claimed, they really are Russian while "purporting" to be Ukrainians. Crimea, after all, was "given" to Ukraine relatively recently by Khrushchev, and the Russians had a fair point in wanting it back. No one seemed to remember the native Crimean Tatars, who had been deported by Stalin and who were in favour of Ukrainian nationality. No one remembered that the Russians had guaranteed Ukraine's borders if Ukraine gave up its nuclear weapons after the fall of the Soviet Union.

When irritated enough by airy dismissals, I'd ask my skeptics on the subject of Ukraine to tell a Scot he was really just English because he speaks that language; to tell an Irishman he isn't Irish at all on the same grounds; to tell them both they were just "confused" Englishmen.

Since the concerns of Eastern Europeans — my concerns — were suspect due to their suspicious Borat-like "exaggeration," I needed to refer to people and places my listeners would take seriously. I could get people's attention by talking about Gotland. First, though, I had to explain that Gotland was an island in the Baltic owned by Sweden. It had demilitarized the island decades ago, but was remilitarizing it after the invasion of Crimea because of the Russian threat.

In other words, Canadians I spoke with took as real, or legitimate, the actions of Sweden because Sweden, I suppose, is somehow part of "us," the West, a "serious" country. What the Baltics, Poland, and others in the region thought about Russia was discounted because they were all East, which is to say, not "us." They were tainted by the stain of Borat, although Borat himself was supposed to have come from Kazakhstan.

When the further Russian invasion of Ukraine took place in February 2022, I sensed some of the same skepticism about Ukraine's situation until Finland and Sweden began to move toward joining NATO. And even now, I have heard ambivalent comments about Ukraine's fight for independence by references to Ukraine's "unfortunate" past, which is code for the ugly war years and the Holocaust. And I sense from this that the unfortunate past of all of Eastern Europe makes the place somehow unworthy of freedom in the present. If one adds the common accusation of corruption, I could note that people seem to have adored *The Godfather* movies but would never claim a country like Italy should be shunned for its own versions of corruption. Tuscany is too beautiful for armchair moralists to tar parts of the country as merely corrupt.

I should mention that Eastern Europeans themselves often don't like to be called "Eastern Europeans," although I've referred to them this way throughout this text. The designation has fallen out of favour because it carries with it the impression of dour, grey stereotypes. No one seems to want to admit to having come from Eastern Europe anymore. Everyone wants to be Central European, or Nordic, or some such. So much so that there has appeared a new book called *Goodbye Eastern Europe*, by Jacob Mikanowski. It's a fascinating history of the last thousand years of the region and it addresses some of the haughty Western attitudes I've mentioned here, using negative terms such as "wog" and "Borat." Unbothered by the label, I continue to use "Eastern Europe" to refer to the places that used to be behind the Iron Curtain, which is now the memory of a metaphor, but still a useful one.

IT FELT STRANGE TO ENTER the Lithuanian Parliament Buildings again in 2017 as the Canadian member of an advisory committee. I had last been in these halls decades earlier as a journalist during the collapse of the Soviet Union, interviewing Vytautas Landsbergis while the country was under perpetual threat of attack by Soviet forces. A memorial to that time lay outside the buildings, a remnant of the construction of concrete blocks intended to defend the site from attack. A fence now stood outside the main entrance because during the upheavals of the past, crowds had tried to storm the buildings.

The fight for Lithuanian independence from the Soviet Union all felt so long ago, especially since Lithuania was now a member of NATO. But peace in Lithuania always feels more tentative than peace in Canada. Lithuania did not have massive Russian immigration after the war, as was the case in Estonia and Latvia. Still, Russia continued to glower beyond the horizon.

Lithuanian problems tended to be domestic. Primary among them was the huge emigration of Lithuanians, hundreds of thousands who had left for better prospects abroad in the UK, Ireland, Spain, or elsewhere. It sometimes felt that the people who fought so hard to be free had taken their freedom and fled to other countries.

The committee I sit on is really best served by lawyers and constitutional experts, so as a novelist, I sometimes feel like an illiterate among the jurists. I felt this most acutely when I was delegated to curate a session on cyber-security. I pulled it off somehow, and didn't see too many smiles in the boardroom as I presented my talk.

Subjects like cyber-security and constitutional law are beyond my range of expertise, obviously. I try to contribute by focusing on subjects such as Lithuania's image abroad, something that could use some help, largely on the subject of the Holocaust. Controversies still rage, with one camp claiming Lithuania has not come sufficiently to terms with its collaborator past, and others claiming the sufferings under Soviet communism are being whitewashed by globalists and Soviet apologists.

The Lithuanian Parliament Buildings are beige brutalist concrete curiosities that sit right beside the neoclassical National Library, a place where I feel more at home. When I am in Vilnius for committee work, I will first wander the halls of the library, nosing through books, and then eventually head for a far less august place.

It's a bookstore called Books for Everyone, over by the crumbling but magnificent yellow-brick market. The poorly signed bookstore up a steep set of stairs has atrocious lighting. Boxes and boxes of unsorted books are stacked among the badly organized shelves. The shelves themselves go right down to the floor, and if I crouch to look for titles there, my arthritic knees pain me sharply as I try to rise. I keep intending to bring a collapsible footstool upon which to perch, but I always forget and I always leave with aching knees.

But the books I find there are priceless, half-hidden windows into the everyday sufferings of people in the twentieth century, sometimes under Soviet rule, and sometimes all the way back to the misery under czarist rule. That bookstore is as much my focus of activity as the Lithuanian Parliament Buildings, maybe more. Contemporary Lithuania will continue to develop contemporary problems, but the past lies fixed in those books, some of them history and some of them fictions, from the various zeitgeists of the past.

sixteen

Reflections Toward
a Hill of Cherry Trees

ON MARCH 10, 2020, I LANDED IN VILNIUS JUST BEFORE the announcement that our Lithuanian parliamentary committee meetings were cancelled due to the impending threat of a pandemic. I should have seen what was coming because the plane from Toronto was half-empty and Chopin Airport in Warsaw, where I changed flights, felt as if it were populated by post-apocalyptic remnants.

I carried on blithely as if the world were not changing under my feet. On Saturday afternoon, March 13, I ate lunch in a Vilnius Vietnamese restaurant along with families watching a parade with marching bands as it moved sprightly down the main street.

On Sunday, news hit the airwaves that a two-week quarantine lockdown was coming. I sped to the airport to postpone my flight back to Canada until after the closure.

Little did I know.

By Monday I was stranded in Vilnius. All flights in or out of Lithuania were cancelled indefinitely. The streets emptied except for a crush around the supermarkets where people were buying food and searching for surgical masks, few of which were to be had. In Canada, people were apparently stocking up on toilet paper, but Lithuania has seen a lot of war and its resulting famine, so people here bought up all the available buckwheat. We don't eat much buckwheat in Canada, but this pseudo-grain, also called kasha, has a lot of protein and a lot of nutritional punch for its weight. Canadians were thinking of clean bums; Lithuanians were thinking of empty stomachs.

The few people I saw in Vilnius tended to cross the street if I was going to walk by them on the sidewalk. I felt I needed to do something, but everybody was supposed to stay home. I felt trapped and restless.

After a couple of days, I rented a car. This is funny in retrospect, because what was I going to do with that car, drive to Canada? Even driving within Europe was restricted and borders were closing to travellers. Later, during the extreme Covid restrictions, even travel between Lithuanian municipalities was forbidden.

Still, I kept a rental car at the curb for a couple of weeks. I took it for a daily spin around the old town of Vilnius. However useless the car was in real terms, it was a consolation as a sort of magical-thinking escape vehicle.

But escape to where? Every place had closed down. There was no escape unless into the past, and that was a place you couldn't reach with a car. Like everyone else, I pretty much stayed inside and looked out the window. Luckily, I had a comfortable ground-floor apartment that faced a courtyard where pigeons strutted and a couple of the trees were beginning to show buds.

The early spring weather was fine and I saw no need to stay indoors if there was no one around except for the occasional police car with officers making sure the rare person on the streets was wearing a mask.

Some people felt anxiety, I learned, and some were depressed. I just felt a sort of stillness descend on me, like the stillness in a theatre after the lights have come down but the curtain hasn't risen yet.

There was plenty of time to think. I considered that *The Decameron* was a ribald and amusing collection of stories set in a time of plague. What better to do than think of something else if every day seemed dreary and fraught with vague danger? So I decided I would write something light and settled into working on a novel I would call *The Seaside Café Metropolis*, set in a boho cafe in Vilnius during the 1950s. A real Soviet-era Vilnius cafe, the Café Neringa, was my model, a place where intellectuals and artists had hung out in a "free" space. Who knew the bread baskets were wired to devices for the KGB listening post in the basement? I also loved the story of the cynical young bohemians in the opera *La bohème*, so I borrowed them for my work.

My son, his ex, and my grandson Feliksas were still in Vilnius then, so — semi-legally, given the restrictions — I took the boy for a few hours each day to give the parents a break, and together he and I played "balloon ball" indoors and I tutored him in French.

But even with a lively grandson and a novel in progress, I was restless, so I devoted myself to walking the empty city. It is filled with baroque churches, and depending on where you stand, you can see as many as five spires at a time.

My apartment was just above the medieval city centre, a steep hike up Basanavičiaus Street, whose stately early-twentieth-century apartment buildings had been half destroyed by fire during liberation at the end of the Second World War. There are still bullet marks across some of the buildings. On one corner there is a bronze sculpture of a boy eating a rubber galosh while looking up wistfully to an apartment window. The statue is a homage to Romain Gary, a Vilnius-born French novelist who wrote a story of a lovestruck boy who promised to eat his shoe if a girl who lived behind one of the apartment windows loved him back.

If there is a charming story on this street, there are brutal ones as well. Just down the way from the bronze boy the street changes its name to Trakų, and on the second floor of a house on this narrow street, a mother of six named Stefanija Ladigienė sheltered a Jewish girl named Irena Veisaitė during the German occupation.

The Soviets had been there first and they would eventually return. Stefanija's husband had been a chief of staff with the Lithuanian armed forces, and for this "crime" he was arrested, jailed, and executed by the Soviets during their first occupation. Then the Germans came and most Jews were killed, while some hid or fled, and Stefanija took in Jewish Irena. As the city was liberated from the Germans, the Soviets returned and Stefanija Ladigienė was deported to the gulag in Irkutsk for the "crime" of being the wife of a man executed by the Soviets. Never mind she had so many children. Never mind she had saved Irena Veisaitė.

I came to know Irena in her old age. She spoke warmly about the woman who had saved her. Not many Jews survived the war in Vilnius, and many of those who did emigrated to better places. But Irena stayed on and studied to be a Germanist. I ran into her frequently at concerts and Santara conferences, and any time I was giving a talk, whether at the Vilnius Book Fair or at the Thomas Mann Festival in the seaside resort of Nida. At that festival, I saw her using a hand rail to pull herself slowly up a hill to the Lutheran church for a concert. She was ninety-one years old. She declined my help, but admitted that the years were slowing her down.

Lithuania in general and Vilnius in particular are full of these kinds of stories of terrible suffering and occasional redemption. On the main street where I had watched a parade stands a building where the names of anti-Soviet resisters who were executed inside are etched into the side wall. Up on Vytenio Street, a nearby suburb where I rented my car, a peculiar sign among the office buildings apologizes because Jewish gravestones had once been used to fence the low-rise commercial yard.

One of my favourite cafes lies in the heart of what was the larger Jewish ghetto, from which thousands went to die. One of the women in another nearby ghetto, Sara Ginaite-Rubinson, escaped, fought as a Jewish partisan, and eventually moved to Toronto where she lived until her death. We spoke together about her history at a conference on the Holocaust in Lithuania.

So many people with tragic or heroic stories, so much history under one's feet. The more you dig, the more stories come up: at the presidential palace, Czar Aleksander I held a ball just days before Napoleon entered the city. Napoleon himself moved in once the czar had fled. Later, some soldiers of Napoleon's army were hacked to pieces on nearby streets at the end of their disastrous retreat from Moscow. History doesn't stop. In July of 2023, during a NATO summit, President Joe Biden was received in the same building by President Gitanas Nausėda of Lithuania.

As I rambled daily along the almost empty streets and spring progressed, I noticed the two cherry trees in my courtyard beginning to blossom. I thought I'd cross the Neris river that separates old Vilnius from its more modern extension and look at the twin columns of cherry trees that line the walk up a pleasant hill to the National Art Gallery. But the authorities did not want people gathering anywhere at all, even outside, and the cherry trees were blocked off with a temporary fence, their blossoms unable to show themselves to admirers except from a distance.

What to do next? Each day I would walk the nearly-empty city to visit one or another of its remarkable buildings and historic sites, from the last tower of the medieval defensive wall to the closed Pushkin memorial museum overlooking a pond in the remains of the Markutis manor park; from the Rasų cemetery where the heart of the Polish leader Józef Piłsudski and Lithuania's father of independence Jonas Basanavičius are buried to an abandoned Soviet-era sports centre that lies upon a Jewish graveyard. I went back home to write a few more paragraphs of my novel in progress and to wait for Global Affairs Canada eventually to find me and other strays. They flew us out six weeks later to Amsterdam, to search out our own ways home from there.

And in the meantime, since I could not go to see the cherry trees on the hill by the National Gallery, I watched the scraggly pair outside my window shed their anonymity and bring spots of colour into the otherwise drab courtyard where the indifferent pigeons strutted.

seventeen
A Little History

LET'S BEGIN WITH A FLASHBACK TO LITHUANIA AROUND
the time of the Second World War for some historical
context.

The Soviets first occupied Lithuania, along with Estonia and Latvia, the other two Baltic States, in June 1940.

Dates will become significant here. Under the Molo-
tov-Ribbentrop Pact of 1939, the Soviet Union had become an ally of Nazi Germany. The two powers agreed
Lithuania was to be absorbed by the USSR and the independent Lithuanian state was dissolved. Soviet repression began almost immediately. Many arrests of former
politicians, the opposition, and high-ranking civil ser-
vants took place right away. Then came the first mass
deportation of over seventeen thousand people, whole
families from whom the men were separated, from May
22 until June 20, 1941. Who were these people? Perceived
potential enemies, but further down the ladder of hier-
archy.

What stopped the deportations? On June 21, 1941, the
Germans invaded, interrupting the Soviet process of

mass repression. Then the Holocaust in Lithuania began with lightning speed and ferocity. When the Soviets returned in 1944, most of the Jews were dead and the arrests and deportations of Lithuanians resumed.

To summarize, the Baltics were occupied three times: first by the Soviets, then by the Germans, and finally, for decades, by the Soviets again. Some people suffered under one or another occupation, and some suffered under more than one.

So the cattle cars bound for Soviet prison camps were being loaded with Lithuanians, with Jews among them too, when the Nazis invaded in 1941. The country was already in crisis, but it was going to get worse. It wasn't even a country anymore. It was first a territory administered by the Soviets and then one administered by the Germans.

Many Lithuanian families were affected in some way by the Soviet deportations. A family on Snaige's side was deported and the father died in the gulag while the wife and mother suffered terribly before their escape.

My father avoided deportation in 1940. He was in hiding since small town policemen were among the types the Soviets were arresting. My mother, a high school teacher at the time, was secretly informed she was on the list for deportation and would soon need to "disappear" to save herself. My uncle Antanas, an opponent of the former independent government, was not so lucky and spent a year being beaten regularly in prison.

Why? An opponent of one regime might turn out to be an opponent of another regime. These types of people "needed" to be repressed. When the Germans invaded, the Soviets retreated with some prisoners and shot others, yet took the time to torture some of them before execution. This detail stuck in the minds of Lithuanians. In a panic to escape, some Soviet officials took a kind of "time out" to peel skin and blind people about to be executed.

My uncle survived by chance, likely in a way similar to the French prisoner Georges Matoré, a writer from the period whose memoir is called *La muselière*. Matoré, and likely my uncle, had cells in Kaunas on a floor too high to reach when the Soviets ran out of time and were retreating in panic.

So my uncle Antanas survived *thanks to the invasion by the Germans*. That same invasion led to the grotesque deaths of the parents of Jewish Aleksandras Štromas and Icchokas Meras.

After his escape, Antanas became involved with a priest helping to rescue Jews. He managed to save three, of whom at least one survived. The saved Jewish boy's father survived too and wrote my uncle a letter of appreciation after the war, and we have all kept copies of this letter as some kind of talisman, some kind of signifier of the goodwill of my uncle Antanas in the horror of the Holocaust.

The USSR returned in 1944, and *thanks to the Soviets*, the small numbers of Jews who were still alive could come out of hiding. When it came to other residents, thanks to the Soviets, tens of thousands more were deported to Siberia, among them another one of my uncles, the farmer, who died sick and despondent there in 1955.

What a terrible history.

LITHUANIANS FOUGHT the Russian Bolsheviks from 1918 until 1920 to create an independent country after the First World War. When in 1940 the Soviet Union incorporated Lithuania by force, many functionaries who had held high positions in the independent government were executed. Others were deported. As mentioned above, the Soviets returned in 1944. Many Lithuanians, among them my parents, fled. Some Lithuanian partisans who stayed behind fought for about a decade with underground resistance, but the movement was crushed over time. And yet, as was evident in the late 1980s, the spirit of resistance was never extinguished.

Lithuania's historical enmity toward and fear of Russia were assuaged when the country joined the EU and NATO, effectively turning the nation west. But the Putin regime's invasion first of Ukrainian Crimea and then Ukraine proper has reactivated hostility. Neighbouring Belarus is in the pocket of Russia as well. Lithuania has been one of the strongest supporters of Ukraine and has, at this writing, taken in sixty thousand refugees, a large number for a country of just over two-and-a-half million.

Ninety per cent of Lithuania's Jews were slaughtered during the Holocaust. A lot of the killers were Lithuanians. There are all sorts of terrible attributes to the Holocaust in Lithuania. In smaller centres, the Jews were not repressed slowly, but rather gathered together locally and shot on the spot and buried in mass graves.

There are many such sites of Jewish massacre scattered throughout Lithuania. The sites are marked by signs on highways and roads in a similar way that historic or touristic sites are marked, and it is chilling to drive across the country and come upon these Holocaust reminders again and again. There were also major extermination sites at the Ninth Fort outside Kaunas, and the Ponary forest near Vilnius. The Kaunas Lietūkis Garage murders were especially horrific because Jews were beaten, tortured, and killed in the presence of spectators, including mothers with their children.

During the post-war Soviet period, the Holocaust was simply presented as an inseparable part of the suffering of locals, and Jews were not specified.

Official recognition of the part Lithuanians played in the Holocaust came later, and the issue is far from resolved. President Algirdas Brazauskas made an apology to the Israeli Knesset for these crimes in 1995, but this statement was far from the end of the story. Much more research has been done into the Holocaust in Lithuania, and many more accusations of Lithuanian avoidance of responsibility have arisen.

In the late 1980s, during the waning Soviet period when Lithuanians had begun to reach toward independence, it became possible to talk openly about the Lithuanian suffering under the Soviets. Until that time, there was no official recognition of the trauma caused by Moscow. One did not admit to the deportations because to have been deported or to have had a relative deported could affect one's livelihood. You might have found yourself unable to study in university or to hold simple positions, such as sailor, if you or your parents had been deported to remote Soviet regions after the war. In other words, having been a victim of postwar Soviet repression was like a stain on your family record.

However painful Soviet repression was for so many families, some critics now contend that memorials to Lithuanian deportations under Soviet rule are a form of masking the crimes of Lithuanians, or claiming protective victimhood status.

The issue is not restricted to Lithuania, but it is felt acutely there. The Prague Declaration of 2008, initiated in part by the late Václav Havel, refers to the crimes of the Nazi and Soviet regimes — in other words, all suffering under totalitarianism — and this has been perceived by some as a diminishment of the unique character of the Holocaust. The Vilnius Genocide Centre, which depicts the Soviet regime's crimes, has been accused of appropriating the term "genocide" and ignoring or diminishing the story of the Holocaust in Lithuania.

At least two books have been published in the last decade by Lithuanians who discovered their fathers or forefathers were either Nazi collaborators or suspected of such. (See titles by Rita Gabis and Julija Šukys at the end of this book. See also Gary Barwin's recent novel on the subject.) University, parliamentary, and independent researchers are continuing to investigate Lithuania's culpability in this period.

CURRENT POLITICS ARE A MOVING TARGET, but so is history. The past keeps on being reconsidered, as we ourselves know in Canada, where we have been reassessing the names of our streets and universities, our monuments and our traditional heroes. Neither the present nor the past are over in and around Lithuania. I keep forever groping toward an understanding of them.

eighteen

The Hometown is Always There for You

YOU NESTLE INTO YOUR SMALL-TOWN HOME FOR A lifetime, or you spread your wings and fly away to your imagined Emerald City. If you do fly away, what fledgling revisits its nest once it has spread its wings? On the other hand, sometimes your small-town home is in the Emerald City already. And anyway, that city holds less appeal from close up — you've already seen behind the wizard's curtain.

The expatriate Lithuanian community in Toronto built themselves a small town within the big city: a community centre, a couple of parish churches, two summer camps, and more; varied groups from Scouts to folk dancers, basketball teams to choirs. As we aging boomers slouch toward extinction, both a Lithuanian retirement home and a nursing home beckon, to say nothing for a moment of the exquisite cemetery in Mississauga where most of our parents now lie.

I can be "away" from this Lithuanian small town or "in" it within fifteen minutes from my West End home.

For our parents, it was a comforting world to inhabit after the trauma and loss of the Second World War. The particularity of Eastern European immigrants was that unlike the Irish or the Italians, they could never go home. So they made themselves at home here, and provided an optional second home for my generation.

And I can take up that option whenever I please.

I was once asked by a magazine to describe Toronto for visitors. This was a high-end literary journal, which I imagined wanted the know about the coolest spots in town. But I chose to interpret the question differently. Here is their question and my answer:

Are there hidden cities within this city that have intrigued or seduced you?

There are two types of hidden cities in this town, but only one of them is accessible to outsiders. The first consists of the vast variety of ethnic neighborhoods, some famous and others not. There are still Italians and Portuguese in their Little Italies and Little Portugals, but there were Jews and Irish and Germans who came before them and left no trace. Millennial moms in sunglasses fill those former ethnic neighbourhoods on weekdays. Kensington Market is still called the Jewish Market by some old-timers. There are still some old synagogues there, but the Jews moved uptown. Behind them they left a warren of dry goods stores, butchers, and fish shops staffed by more recent immigrants, some of them Caribbean.

These are the hidden cities that are not really hidden at all. You just have to walk the town to find them.

The second type of secret city is also ethnic and religious, but it contains a world sealed to the outsider, and anyway, it contains secrets no hipster would ever care to explore. There are many immigrants both recent and old in this city, and they maintain various types of community centres. In one of the Lithuanian parishes there is a small library with about ten thousand books read by almost no one. The librarian says she serves primarily me, and when I ask her when a book is due, she waves her hand dismissively.

In these volumes left by my parents' generation are the stories of being locked up in the Stutthof concentration camp for resisting the Nazis, of deportations to Siberia for no crimes at all, of Jews murdered and saved, of a children's writer who went on to become the Dr. Seuss of Lithuania only after ingratiating himself by shooting dead two resistance partisans. Dramatic and heartbreaking stories that almost no one will notice. I know for certain that such forgotten libraries and archives exist in Latvian and Estonian community centres, and probably in dozens more.

These are the true secrets of Toronto. These are the stories of what brought people here. Almost no one will ever know them because they seem quaint, parochial, banal. These hidden cities keep their secrets in plain sight, but no one is looking.

FOR MY GENERATION, the local Lithuanian community is
something like a drop-in centre, especially around certain dates.

FOR SOME EASTERN EUROPEANS, the cult of the dead fits in
comfortably with contemporary life. The annual memorial day is not quite as dramatic as the Day of the Dead
in Mexico, nor as dramatic in Canada as in Lithuania.
There, on All Saints' Day, in the Rasų cemetery in Vilnius,
visitors fill the graveyard and set candles on the graves
and sometimes sing hymns or other songs. It's a beautiful and moving festival of the dead.

As a Lithuanian journalist pointed out to me, the Baltic and Eastern European attitude toward the dead is not
like the Celtic one, which fears ghosts roaming the night
to haunt the living. Instead, the Baltic view is that when
your dead come out, you welcome them. They are your
people.

The late Lithuanian poet Sigitas Geda explained that
the Lithuanian word for "flag," *vėliava*, is based on the
word for soul. When you went into battle in the past, you
brought this flag with you not only to show your banner,
but to have your dead with you in order to swell your
numbers on the field.

Halloween is October 31, All Saints' Day is November
1, and All Souls' Day is November 2. In Lithuania, November 1 is a national holiday and in my childhood, Catholic

schools celebrated this day as a holiday too. We smarmy Catholic kids would fill our pockets with candy collected the night before and then parade ourselves outside the chain link fences of the Protestant schools, eating our candy to demonstrate our superiority over the unfortunate non-Catholic kids who had to sit in class and watch us until their vice-principal chased us away.

A kind of relic of the cemetery-visiting tradition exists at the Lithuanian parish and cemetery in Mississauga, west of Toronto. When I was a child, the place was still full of old apple orchards being cleared for new suburbs, which now surround this burial ground with its varied monuments that range from kitsch to fine art. I've been going to that cemetery on the Sunday closest to All Souls' since I was five or six years old.

The big parish hall stays open all afternoon, serving Lithuanian foods such as potato kugel, heavy enough, or massive dumplings called "zeppelins," meat inside potato dough. They are the size of your fist and covered with a gravy of bacon, onions, and sour cream and they are filling enough to satisfy your belly for a day and a half. There might be an art or history exhibition in the Lithuanian archive nearby, or a table with imported breads and preserves for sale. People will go to Mass or not, but almost everyone who comes to visit the graves of their dead will stay a while to eat, and then go out to light a candle at a family cemetery monument.

This is the time and place where my daytime ghosts accumulate. They are not the dead, who lie calmly out in the field, but the Lithuanian children of my ethnic childhood of decades ago. Johnny from down the street, my once-upon-a-time best friend, whose father died young and who my parents would invite up to the cottage, to let him get out of town. Vida, who married a provincial parliamentarian turned wine maker and whose parents "scandalously" sent her to the closer public school instead of the more distant Catholic school. There will be many I meet in the parish hall or out in the windy cemetery, old men and women who remember my name and many whose names I've forgotten. Folk dance partners of the past, girls I kissed, classmates from the boring Lithuanian Saturday school grammar lessons, where we threw paper airplanes and made jokes so cruel that our young language teacher burst into tears.

This big church hall, with its all-day meal for second- and third-generation Lithuanians, is a transit lounge. We carry the memories of our parents whom we will visit in their graves after we eat, and many of us will eventually end up in the field outside, lying among them. They had hoped to be buried in their home country, but modified that former desire, and lie instead in the ground where their children set down roots.

SOME ECHOES of the past exist in other places too. Like my parents, many Lithuanians who established themselves in and around Toronto began to buy or build summer cottages. The more outdoorsy types ended up around Waubaushene and Honey Harbour to fish and to hunt, and the more conventional ones bought places at a stretch of Wasaga Beach on Georgian Bay. It must have been an ethnic habit of the time: not only to settle close to one another, but to holiday together too. The Ukrainians tended to buy around Cawaja Beach, the Poles at Balm Beach, and the Estonians near Sunset Beach by Collingwood.

Near our family cottage at Wasaga Beach there were two summer camps, a Lithuanian deli, and a summer parish where the priest threw a picnic on his name day, one that drew hundreds. As a side of beef sizzled on a spit, men drank secretly from liquor bottles stashed in their wives' beach bags, because drinking at picnics was outlawed in Ontario.

That is all in the past, but when Snaige and I aged past canoe camping and holidaying off the grid, we bought her old family cottage at Wasaga Beach. There are still several dozens of cottages owned by people like us, the ones who remember our immigrant childhoods. But as the "English" watched our parents fill the cottages, so now we see the beach filling with different new Canadians, often South Asians who have been here long enough to start looking for summer places of their own.

Wasaga was a consolation to parents who could not get to Lithuania's Baltic seaside as they had in summers before the war. Now, our generation can summer on the Baltic if we want to. Or we might just want to walk on the beach at Wasaga, to watch a sunset or to see our grandchildren splash around the shallow shoreline.

THESE VISITS to the Lithuanian-tinctured past, either at the parish, the cemetery, or the beach, are all optional. You believe nostalgia and memory are sentimental traps? No problem. Stay away. Toronto and Canada and the whole world are all full of other options. Take them if you want. Or drop by at some version of a small Lithuanian town within the metropolis. Eat something. Lithuanians don't like to send people away hungry.

nineteen

As for Me and My Place

BEFORE THE SOVIET UNION BEGAN TO COLLAPSE, Lithuania was invisible on the world stage and it was largely invisible to me outside the small circle of family and émigré society. Our parents had tried to hammer home Lithuanian history, and so had our Saturday schools. They tried to make us read classic Lithuanian writers such as Vincas Krėvė Mickevičius or poet Kristijonas Donelaitis. But Lithuanian literature, either Soviet or expatriate, was remote for me. We didn't really read anything from Lithuania, so I and my generation might as well have been living in an expatriate *oral* culture, except for a few women who seemed to thrive on Lithuanian poetry.

English was our strongest language, but looking for English books about our part of the world was like looking for guidebooks to mythical locations.

As I have said, Czesław Miłosz "legitimized" the subject of Eastern Europe in general, and Poland and Lithuania in particular, and provided texts now translated into English.

Miłosz was ironic about the remoteness of his childhood world from the eyes of Western Europe, but he was certain of the place's importance. For him, life in the Lithuanian countryside shed some light on the broader world.

Miłosz's picture of his childhood environs had deep meaning for me. In his work, not only was the natural world evoked, but also the folk culture of the region, where devils still roamed the countryside during Mass to take to hell those who had not gone to church.

Miłosz articulated the sense of invisibility I had grown up with. Not only Lithuania suffered from invisibility — so did the entirety of Eastern Europe, including Poland and the Baltics, Belarus and Ukraine. Historian Kate Brown expressed this sense in her book on the borderland between Russia and Poland, aptly titled *A Biography of No Place*. She even refers to the gift of marginality as a way of studying a place through neither a nationalistic lens nor one of empire. Some gift, one might say.

Miłosz took the chip off my shoulder about coming out of Eastern Europe. Rather than feeling less serious because of my family's origins, I felt after reading him that I came from a country freighted with historical meaning and also one capable of producing great art. He wrote in *The Captive Mind* that the Eastern European might look down on the Westerner for his naïveté:

… the man of the East cannot take Americans seriously because they have never undergone the experiences that teach men how relative their judgments and thinking habits are. Had the Westerner stumbled upon a corpse on the street, he would have called the police. A crowd would have gathered, and much talk and comment would have ensued. Now the Easterner knows he must avoid the dark body lying in the gutter, and refrain from asking unnecessary questions …

Then, decades later, came Anne Applebaum, author of important histories on the gulag and the Iron Curtain. She reinforced Eastern Europe as a topic worthy of consideration. Reviewing *Bloodlands* by Timothy Snyder, perhaps the best-known historian of Eastern Europe in English, Applebaum said this:

Miłosz's bitter analysis did not go far enough. Almost sixty years after the poet wrote those words [about the Westerner], it is no longer enough to say that we West-erners lack imagination. Timothy Snyder, a Yale historian whose past work has ranged from Habsburg Vienna to Stalinist Kiev, takes the point one step further. In *Blood-lands*, a brave and original history of mass killing in the twentieth century, he argues that we still lack any real knowledge of what happened in the eastern half of Eu-rope in the twentieth century. And he is right: if we are American, we think "the war" was something that start-ed with Pearl Harbor in 1941 and ended with the atomic bomb in 1945. If we are British, we remember the Blitz of 1940 (and indeed are commemorating it energetically this year) and the liberation of Belsen. If we are French, we remember Vichy and the Resistance. If we are Dutch we think of Anne Frank. Even if we are German we know only a part of the story.

Most Canadians of a certain age, she could have added, probably lean toward the British view.

Ignorance about Eastern Europe has decreased a great deal over the last few decades. The work of other important writers such as Norman Davies, historian of both Poland and Europe, and the late Tony Judt no longer permits us to call the region terra incognita. Add the writing of Marci Shore and Sherhii Plokhy and the sources become ever richer. Eastern Europe is still peripheral, of course, in the popular Western mind, but not to those with some interest in history. Norman Naimark, author of *Stalin's Genocides,* is worth singling out for his use of the term "genocide," which has become controversial, as any seeker of the word's definition on the internet will find.

Naimark points out that the man who developed the definition of genocide, Raphael Lemkin, first thought of that kind of massive crime as "barbarity," and wanted the definition to include not only the murder of religious or national groups but social ones as well. The Soviets resisted this definition because they were in the habit of repressing the intelligentsia as a means of cutting off the "head" of a state in order to control it. Thus the murder of the Polish officers in Katyn could be described as a genocide and, one might add, so could the deportation of almost seventeen thousand Lithuanians in June 1941, a week before the German invasion of the Soviet Union, in particular if one adds the hundred thousand more who were deported after the war.

On this issue, I think no one has the right to own a term. On the other hand, use it too often and we might soon see its impact disappear. But who is going to referee the use of these terms? Nobody. One applies the definition as one sees fit.

Familiarity with contemporary literary writing about Eastern Europe has continued to expand as well. Witness Svetlana Alexievich, the Belarusian writer who won the Nobel Prize for writing, among other subjects, about the Belarusian villages inhabited solely by women and children after the loss of so many men in the Second World War. Another notable writer from the region gaining ever more interest in Canada is Olga Tokarczuk of Poland, winner of both the Nobel and Booker Prizes. And there is rising attention being paid to the Finnish-Estonian writer Sofi Oksanen, whose novel *When the Doves Disappeared* describes a character who collaborated both with the Nazis and the communists.

Eastern Europe has become a place rich in both fiction and non-fiction accessible to the English-speaking world.

CANADA'S CONTRIBUTION to writing about Eastern Europe is still developing. In the first decade of the twenty-first century, I began to have occasional lunches with Eva Stachniak, a Canadian writer who immigrated here from Poland in the 1980s and has gone on to become a best-selling author of English-language historical novels set in both Eastern and Western Europe. We talked about a subject that I'd wondered about for some time. Why did Canada, with inhabitants of Ukrainian heritage numbering 1.3 million, and of Polish heritage numbering 1.1 million, have so little literature about those places?

There are some prominent writers of Ukrainian and Polish heritage — Eva herself, Janice Kulyk Keefer, Myrna Kostash, and others — but not as many as I would expect. There is, however, a Ukrainian Canadian literary prize, the KOBZAR Book Award, to help promote Ukrainian-Canadian writing.

In conversation with Eva, I theorized that immigrants from Eastern Europe might have felt less self-confident than immigrants from the British Isles or the Commonwealth, with their English-language heritage. Perhaps this is true. In my childhood, I felt a sense of unworthiness, but when I brought up this thesis with Canadian writer David Bezmozgis, of Latvian and Jewish heritage and over twenty years my junior, he found my sense of unworthiness unfamiliar, even curious. Maybe it's just generational. He did add later that he always felt he was writing from within a Jewish literary tradition.

The need of Eastern Europeans to be taken seriously, to be considered "Western," existed during the Soviet era. There was even a line of thought that held Moscow, the inheritor of the Mongol Golden Horde, to be antagonistic to the West and Western ideas. This used to be considered a marginal, almost racist belief, one held by a fringe, but Keir Giles recently wrote in *Russia's War on Everybody* that he shares the belief that Russia's culture admires strength and power rather than democracy. Thus it is a permanent regional threat. Those Eastern Europeans might have had it right all along.

twenty

Remembering and Forgetting

THIS BINATIONAL LIFE OF MINE INVOLVES A LOT OF living in the past, scratching it until it becomes like a sore you shouldn't touch. More than once I have felt sated and bored with everything Lithuanian that I was reading and writing about. So I took the opportunity of an invitation to give an address on the subject of this "memory fatigue" at the Thomas Mann Festival in Nida, Lithuania, in the summer just before Covid.

Nida is a former fishing village on the Curonian spit, a kind of long, thin sandbar that runs from the mainland between a vast lagoon on one side and the Baltic Sea on the other. In Nida, up on a hill, Thomas Mann had his summer house for a few years, until the Nazis took power and he fled. The picturesque village of Nida is now primarily a summer resort. It faces the lagoon side of the Curonian Spit. The old fishermen's houses look like Viking dwellings, and the moderate difficulty of getting there limits the number of tourists. Not far from Mann's house on the hill is a red-brick Lutheran church where concerts are held during the festival.

When I was there, if I had free time, I could walk for half an hour across the spit from the town of Nida to see the broad beaches facing the Baltic Sea.

It may have been naïve of me to choose such a place to talk about imaginary homelands, the advantage of forgetting. But I thought I was on to something.

Here is what I said, some of which I've touched on earlier in this narrative:

MY FAMILY IN CANADA grew up in perhaps the best place and time for people like us, when the economy was expanding and no wars were being fought on our land. We were like survivors of a shipwreck, people who landed on a paradisiacal shore, the Swiss Family Robinson with a refrigerator and a car. We were foreigners, but unremarkable among many other European immigrants. Millions died and millions fled; millions were displaced like pieces recut to form a new jigsaw puzzle.

But for all of its wonders, for all of its wealth, Weston, Ontario, was not my homeland, even though it is where I was born and grew up, a place which I remember so fondly to this day — outside, the smell of cut grass lawns and the sound of young men washing their cars for Saturday night dates; inside, the sound of the vacuum cleaner bumping against the baseboards by the carpet and the smell of bacon and eggs being fried for lazy weekend boys.

The immigrants of that time were called Displaced Persons, or DPs for short, and I somehow remained profoundly displaced in the land of my birth.

Consider the work of Salman Rushdie, who has written about imaginary homelands too, although his book of essays has to do mostly with post-colonialism and Britain. I take an important observation from Rushdie. In his view, the migrant is the central or defining figure of the twentieth century. Tantalizingly, Rushdie also writes that "we live in ideas and through images we seek to comprehend the world."

In my writing, I focus on European homelands. Partially this is a reflex, an unthinking action. But beyond that, as a man of European heritage, I feel I have some right to this enquiry as I might not have a right to explore other cultures, or "appropriate" them in current vocabulary.

We should agree with Rushdie that there is nothing remarkable about emigrants of that period. Many if not most of their children managed to assimilate in the places where they landed, often retaining some fondness for their heritage, such as a taste for the food of their parents and grandparents. Provided they were safe, some might even have gone back, at the very least to visit the places their parents came from, such as Ireland or Greece or Italy.

But the fact of the Iron Curtain made going back to Lithuania impossible. It was not merely a question of the

Iron Curtain. Other countries lay behind it too, but the Baltic States, Lithuania among them, had been incorporated into the Soviet Union and thus disappeared from the map.

Imagine, a whole country disappearing! At first, people in the West might have remembered its name, but as time passed, they forgot it existed.

Let me return for a moment to Weston, Ontario, where I entered the world. We children felt displaced there, not only because we came from Lithuania, but because in the dawn of the television era, Weston was so remote from the global centres as to have no meaning in and of itself. For children of the era, television and comic books were our true homes, and the places depicted there were American. Our true homelands lay in the exciting places of adventure like the western ranch on *Bonanza*, or the funny and urbane New York of *The Dick Van Dyke Show*, *The Honeymooners*, and *I Love Lucy*, or the Hollywood of *The Steve Allen Show*. In comics it was Gotham City for Batman, Metropolis for Superman, or again, New York City for the Fantastic Four.

I lived with so many levels of exile I barely existed. Indeed, I felt as if I did not exist at all, or if I did exist, I did not "register" in the world. If someone had told me then that I was a "nobody," I would have bristled but agreed. A young man with parents from nowhere, a place that literally did not exist on the map, lived in a place that was almost nowhere. I was not alone, of course, because the Estonians, Latvians, and Ukrainians felt the same way. We even had our own basketball league, which might as well have been called "The Vanished Nations League."

Everyone needs to be someone, and every someone needs to be someplace. I could solve the problem of my nonexistence by becoming a writer. Proof of my existence would then lie on the page. But I could not easily solve the problem of being someplace. I have been searching for a homeland for most of my life, and frequently it has been a homeland of the imagination.

My first homeland of the imagination lay in the ruins of the British Empire, called in my time the Commonwealth. If a homeland is a place that brings you comfort and security, this imaginary European homeland of England and by extension the Commonwealth consoled me for many things — for being a failure at sports, for living in the godforsaken emptiness of Weston, and for having a father who never really adapted to Canada and a mother who was often very sad. One homeland of the imagination, the English one, was full of bravado and empire. My other, my Lithuanian one, was full of melancholy. These homelands were like two angels on my shoulders, or to be Freudian, my English homeland was my childish superego, and my Lithuanian homeland was my id.

But the English homeland did not last. It was destroyed by the offhand comment of my friend Vaughan's grandmother.

Such a fragile homeland this Commonwealth was! So easy to destroy with an offhand comment! And I should not wring my hands about this comment because it awoke me to the reality of my condition. The Commonwealth was not my homeland, imagined or otherwise. I would need to go looking for my homeland, but from the ruined British homeland I took one prize — namely, the English language. It was the tool I would use to forge myself and to find my own homelands as well.

Well then, what about the homeland my parents had left behind? My mother had bouts of gloom for the loss of it. She spoke repeatedly about the place where her own mother lived until she died in the late 1950s. This very same grandmother once wrote to say how sad she was that she could never meet me because she wished to buy me a bag of candies. To a child, at a time when candies were sold by the pound, a bag of them represented a fortune as well as love, but no one ever bought them for me because my grandmother lived in a land that did not exist.

This homeland of my parents therefore existed for them, but it did not exist outside the walls of our house or the walls of our Lithuanian church or the yard of our Saturday morning Lithuanian school. If my Commonwealth English homeland came to me through its authors, my parents' Lithuanian homeland came to me through the oral recounting of their childhoods.

One of my lost European homelands, the Commonwealth one, was written, and the other homeland, the Lithuanian one, was spoken, but both were imaginary.

I should add that my mother did read me a few stories from Lithuanian books. Two of the stories were by Jonas Biliūnas. The first was called "Brisiaus galas" ("The End of Brisius"), about an old dog who dreams of adventures with his master, only to be shot by this master because the dog is too old. The other story, "Kliudžiau" ("My Error"), was about a boy who takes his bow and arrow and in a moment of bravado shoots and kills a neighbourhood cat, after which he is filled with remorse. A third memorable story, by the poet Justinas Marcinkevičius, was "Grybų karas" ("The War of the Mushrooms"), in which the mushrooms decide to go to war but die of rot before they can execute their plan.

My Canadian friends laugh merrily when I tell them of these Lithuanian children's stories, so dark and so pessimistic compared to the happy tales of Disney.

So what about my parents' homeland? For a long time it could not be mine. Their homelands were both their childhood homes and family, and their youths as well, when they were young and easy and green and carefree. In my own cocky youth, I considered my parents to be nostalgic, and there was no more dismissive term in my adolescent vocabulary. Their memories were not my memories and I was casually cruel about their irrelevance. I would find a homeland, perhaps, but I would find it myself.

If I did not feel Canada was my homeland, and if the Commonwealth would not have me, and dismal Lithuania was not for me either, what was I to do?

My search for a homeland went into the university library where I spent many days and nights when I was a student. I wandered the stacks of the European history section, searching for mentions of the word "Lithuania" in the indexes of European history books. Then I would return to a carrel where I was studying English literature and might be writing a paper on Ernest Hemingway or William Faulkner.

So the language of my abandoned Commonwealth homeland took me to other ones: the Northern Michigan landscape of Hemingway's *The Nick Adams Stories* or the Yoknapatawpha County of Faulkner. These were homelands I occupied for a while, though not European ones, unless perhaps the Italy of Hemingway's *A Farewell to Arms*, a novel whose hopelessness appealed to my youthful nihilism.

That library was a kind of refuge — bookish men, women, and children have found asylum in libraries ever since wars, fractious parents, whining children, moronic television shows, leaf blowers, motorcycles, food processors, and other dangers or irritants have driven them away from the rest of life. Libraries have been celebrated often, notably by Alberto Manguel, who spoke of sitting in his French provincial private library, listening to how the books connected to one another at night.

But the library is not the destination of this voyage of European homelands of the imagination. It is instead a point of departure, a portal. It is the place that takes you to the homelands, whether in fiction or non-fiction because both are imaginary once they are in books and are no longer concrete.

Through it, I might have entered one of Ray Bradbury's homelands, which sound so warm and so strange in *The Martian Chronicles*: "It was quiet in the deep morning of Mars, as quiet as a cool black well, with stars shining in the canal waters, and, breathing in every room, the children curled with their spiders in closed hands, the lovers arm in arm, the moons gone, the torches cold, the stone amphitheaters deserted."

Through that same portal, with so many choices, I might have entered into one of Norman Davies's histories — because Lithuania was not the only place that had disappeared over time. This very fine historian, the author of many volumes but for us most pointedly of *Vanished Kingdoms*, says of the ancient Prussians of the tenth century that they lived on the Amber Coast and their name might have meant something like "Water Tribes" or "People of the Lagoons." Such potential romance in this sort of naming! Such potential for a homeland, but perhaps a little too far back in history.

Why all this going into fantasy or ancient history through libraries when Lithuania gained its independence after the First World War, and thus I could have found it to be my homeland?

Umberto Eco says we know perfectly well the real world exists, but we decide to take the fictional one seriously — let me modify that to say we take the *imaginary* world seriously.

I have taken you on a rambling journey and it wouldn't be fair to leave you without reaching my goal. Through this library portal I did find my European homeland. It remains an imaginary one, an evocative one as strange as the Mars of Ray Bradbury, but so close I feel I inhabit it in my mind if not in my body.

I am speaking of another writer I discovered long ago, namely Czesław Miłosz, who in *The Issa Valley* and *Native Realm* wrote with great love and detail of his childhood home in a crumbling Lithuanian manor house where everyone spoke Polish, the language of his writing too. This landscape of creaking wagons and birdsong among the trees is alive to me. I can smell it and feel it and find comfort in it.

But it is only one part of my European homeland of the imagination. I don't inhabit the world solely of Miłosz, because others have evoked this world as well. I think of Tadas Ivanauskas, the great naturalist of Lithuania, the founder of the Kaunas zoo. In his *Aš apsisprendžiu* (*I Make a Decision*), he writes of a childhood in a manor house where the hunting dogs sprawled wherever they liked, the lamp oil was measured out each evening, and a barrel of vinegar stood in the living room forever because, though no one knew how it got there, since it had stood there since the beginning of time it might as well continue.

There are others who have written well to evoke their landscapes, not just the inhabitants of manor houses — Konstantinas Žukas, in his *Žvilgsnis į praeitį (A Look at the Past)*. In that book, he describes the chaos and brutality of the Russian Revolution when he served as a czarist army officer before fleeing to independent Lithuania. Or Jonas Budrys in his *Kontražvalgyba Lietuvoje (Counter-intelligence in Lithuania),* in which he describes how a small band of insurrectionists managed to seize the city of Memel, rename it Klaipėda, and attach it to Lithuania. There are many other less celebrated but equally engaging writers who have evoked the atmosphere of their Lithuanian homelands.

Their homelands have become mine.

These homelands, like those of my parents, are gone from everywhere but the imagination. Miłosz himself said, upon revisiting his childhood home, that not one stone stood upon another in any recognizable way after the passage of a few disastrous decades. Yet Miłosz, in most of his later prose works, returned again and again to this place because it was the place that had formed him. I who sneered at the nostalgia of my parents learned to respect their views through Miłosz.

But critically, both my parents and Miłosz spoke of memories, whereas I speak of imaginary European places, imaginary in the sense that I never inhabited them in my childhood and they no longer exist now.

These homelands of the imagination are richly described and welcoming, waiting for me and others like me as if they were chairs by the fire on a cold and windy evening. I enter these homelands in my writing and I live in them in my mind. My novels are nothing more than extensions of these memoirs, but my work is written in English. I step into these worlds and I rearrange the furniture to suit my story, and I add or remove characters as I might invite or not invite guests to a party.

I HAVE WRITTEN HERE about one of my own European homelands of the imagination, but there are other potential ones. When I am in the Lithuanian village of Lyneželis near the border and my mobile phone registers Belarus, I think of the homeland evoked by Svetlana Alexievich. Here in Nida when I am out on the Baltic beach, my mobile phone is so close to Kaliningrad that it thinks it is in Russia. Then I think of a long-gone colleague of mine in Canada, Margitta Dinzl, who was carried out of East Prussia in the arms of her mother at the end of the Second World War. She spoke so vividly to me of that place, one she had never seen in adulthood. That was over forty years ago, and I can practically still smell it, yet it existed nowhere else but in her mind and is now seeded in mine. And when I say seeded I mean exactly that. My imagination begins to work on these places, to make them potential zones of comfort for me, and the places begin to grow if I let them.

In her old age, my mother-in-law began to suffer from dementia. She saw ghosts: her dead friend from down the road knocked on her door. What surprised me was another change that came upon her.

She could no longer feel at home. When I rose from her kitchen table in a house she had inhabited for fifty years, she would say to me, "Are you going my way? Do you think you could take me home?" She had begun to disassociate herself from her surroundings. She no longer felt their comfort, their reassuring warmth.

Did she long for her childhood home, the one she had left decades ago? No. I showed her a photo. That was not what she meant. It turns out persons in certain stages of dementia long for a home, but it has ceased to exist as any familiar place. It exists only as an idea.

For her, it was neither the place she was in then nor any place she had ever inhabited before. It was abstract, the *idea* of comfort and familiarity.

She too had an imaginary home, one that was elsewhere, but she could no longer enter into it. She was looking for it because the search for a homeland is a life-long quest. European homelands, even imaginary ones, can slip away. We leave them by choice or memory loss, or because the world of politics and economics erupts and forces us to leave them. But they are not in one fixed place. We seek their comfort, yet this wellbeing can vanish as quickly as a season's end, and we need to migrate with our imagination to find our homelands again.

twenty-one
Then and Now

WHILE VISITING MY RELATIVES IN ŠIAULIAI, A NORTH-
ern Lithuanian city, in 2022, I was standing out in the
yard on a fine day in May and suddenly heard the roar of
two military jets flying off above us. The war in Ukraine
had been going on since earlier that winter.

"Is this the beginning of another war?" I asked my
cousin, believing I was making a small joke.

"Not yet," Virgilija replied. "Those are just a pair of
NATO jets scrambling to head off the Russians. They
probe our airspace all the time."

The Belarusian border was closer than the Russian
border, but that was no consolation because the Belaru-
sians were in Russia's pocket.

She repeated, "Not *yet*."

"So how will you know when it really is war?" I asked
her.

"When five jets shoot up."

She didn't mean to sound ironic. She was just telling
me how it is.

In the summer of 2022, I was digging around a little

more in family history. Cousin Virgilija knew a lot because she was raised by her mother's mother, whose husband, Aleksandras, died in the gulag in Vorkuta in 1955. Virgilija's own mother died young.

Virgilija was the one who could fill in so much murky family background for me. That summer, she let me know cousin Ovidijus had discovered a cache of letters from Aleksandras. This man was my father's brother. The coal-mining Vorkuta prison camp was one of the more notorious camps in the gulag system, and my uncle Aleksandras rotted there until his death because he was convicted of being too successful as a farmer.

After Stalin's death, a partial amnesty was applied to the camp and criminal prisoners with short sentences were released. Not so political prisoners, of whom my uncle was one. There was an uprising in 1953, which was put down when camp guards fired into the protesters, killing sixty-six. I do not know if Aleksandras was involved in that uprising. He survived two more years.

But I do know Aleksandras had fallen ill by then, and he sent a series of letters from the camp, begging his children to help get him amnestied. By an unusual twist of fate, his wife's nephew, Pranas, was sent off to a prison camp as well. Pranas was a man in his twenties, sent to the gulag along with some sort of Lithuanian sports team that had protested against the Soviets. In a letter to his cousin, Virgilija's mother, he describes meeting his uncle Aleksandras, who had been in the gulag for ten years and was in failing health.

Here is a portion of the letter he wrote to Aleksandras's daughter:

1955-06-13

Dear Lione!

You might wonder why you are getting an unexpected letter from me. Maybe you've even forgotten me. It's me, Pranas!

You might ask why, after not having written for so long, I have now decided to send you a letter. Yesterday, that is to say this year (1955), June 12, I happened to be where your dad has been for so long.

After many difficulties, I found the hospital and the ward where he is a patient. Access is restricted, so I went to a window and asked if there wasn't a Šileika in there.

One of the patients went to a bed and roused a sleeping man. I thought this man might just have a similar last name, as often happens, but when the man raised his head, rested it on his hand, sat up and rapidly stepped out of bed, I saw more clearly that it was indeed my uncle.

He was so changed! Ten years of misery and suffering, haven't left much of the man. ... Suddenly, he recognized me, and with eyes full of tears and a trembling voice asked, "Pranas, my boy! How did you end up here?"

What I felt then and what I said, I can't remember. We kissed. The poor man did not know what to do. ...

It was not a happy meeting. He told me about his troubles, his whole story of illness. I listened and I looked at him and asked myself, where was that happy, handsome, joke-loving uncle of mine?

Lione, I don't know if it is worth telling you all of what I saw. His health is very poor. No one cares. …

My God, my God! So much suffering, years of famine, cold, and brutal prison-camp labour. Finally the illness, which has been going on for three years. Terrible, unbearable pain. …

Forgive me, Lione, if I have written too much that will be painful for you. But what to do? Lie? Pray for your father. The almighty will hear your heartfelt prayer.

Goodbye,
Pranas

Time collapses. The war my parents fled seems to be ongoing even now, not far across the border from Lithuania.

The past comes back in disguise, wearing a different mask, but causing chaos of a kind we did not expect to see again in the West. Lithuania is far away, and it is very close by.

When Ma Barker of the Barker–Karpis Gang was asked why she and her boys robbed banks, she said, "Because that's where the money is." A simple answer.

A similar question and a similar answer: Why do I write about Lithuania all the time? Because that's where the stories are.

twenty-two

The Afterlife of the Strato Chief

MY FATHER WAS BOTH SENTIMENTAL AND CHEAP, AND TO him an old car was like a horse that had served the family for decades and deserved to be put out to pasture rather than sold for glue. The automobile equivalent of pasture was a space in our double garage, where we had room because the driveway was long and broad and could accommodate a few visitors. There the old car could rest in its past glory, gathering dust for years. My father would go in every once in a while just to see if the engine still turned over.

As more years passed, the old car at the end of its life would transform itself in my father's mind. He'd come to think of it as a very good car that was just put aside for a while. In his mind, the Strato Chief, retired about 1968 at the age of ten, had been reinvigorated by its rest and was ready to go back into service around 1975.

Somehow, my father managed to convince his sons that this ridiculous proposition was true. I checked the oil in the car, topped it up, got a license plate and drove it around the block a couple of times. It seemed OK. Maybe my father was right, even though a bent piece of a Meccano toy set was used to hold one of the front headlights in place and you could see through the body in a couple of rusted-out spots.

In a burst of enthusiasm, I cleaned up the inside. It was worn, but serviceable, because we'd had plastic wrap over the upholstery for the first five years of the car's life. During those years, we'd burned short-panted legs against the infernal plastic in the summer, and suffered the stiffness of it under our bums in the winter.

Having started the engine and cleaned up the inside, I next wanted to renew the car by taking it through a car wash. The windows and even the panels leaked in many places, and I was hit not only by drips but more powerful streams of water that soaked me from all sides: from the holes in the floor, from the imperfectly closed windows, and even from the rotten seals around the windscreen.

Even this cold shower did not dampen the enthusiasm my father had instilled in me. I proposed that my middle brother, Joe, join me in a trip across town to visit our oldest brother, Andy, who lived in an eastern suburb at the time. Even deluded as we were, we had brains enough not to get on the highway. We took Sheppard Avenue, which ran across the top of Toronto through an endless variation of suburban sprawl.

Our clean but rusty car managed well until it came to the valley at the upper Don River. It glided down the long hill, but no amount of encouragement could get it up the other side. The car really was like an old horse that could still make it downhill but not uphill. Nor could it return the way it had come, because from the bottom of the valley, both directions were "up."

We called Andy, who arrived with a thick rope, and we towed the car back to our home where my aging father met us, heartbroken. He could not bear to watch the heap being towed away for scrap.

So WHAT OF THE FUTURE that car heralded, with its stars on the rear panels?

Sixty years later, we live not quite in the world of the Jetsons, but like a happy few, in terms of the whole world, we live a lucky life.

Three decades after independence, my remaining relatives in Lithuania live reasonably comfortable lives — if not on par with those in a country with a GDP like Canada's, then certainly better than many other places.

What's been achieved?

It's the wrong question. History doesn't achieve anything. Some say it arcs toward freedom and some say it is cyclical, but the only certainty is that things never remain the same. War looms in the East again as time continues its relentless flow.

Some look to the future and some look to the past. And then there are people like me, stuck in the eddies, moving neither further along nor back, lost in contemplation in the complexities of time and geography.

And as for Tony, it turns out he was not entirely dead, just absent most of the time. Today, if I am waiting in line for fast food and they ask me what name to call when the food is ready, I tell them Tony. It's simpler that way, and besides, I don't have anything to prove anymore.

twenty-three

A Moving Target

CANADIAN WRITER SHEILA HETI ASKS IN THE TITLE OF one of her books, "How should a person be?" Initially, I found it an annoying title, a falsely naïve phrase. It posed the question as if geography and history and social station are irrelevant to some sort of tabula rasa being, this *person*, perhaps one sitting on a stool in a food court in a mall, or leaning intensely close to a stranger at a crowded party after too many drinks and a certain amount of weed.

Do I sound irritated?

I certainly was, but her question really deserves thought, and her phrasing makes fresh the old questions of what makes the good life, what makes the virtuous life.

What does asking this question assume? A certain kind of freedom one has, options one can choose from if one has the good fortune to live relatively well in Canada now, or in a similar place and at a certain time. If you don't need to struggle to *be* in the first place, you can decide *how* you should be.

I was struck by Carolyn Abraham's study of genealogy, called *The Juggler's Children*. In that book, among many other observations, she makes the point that all of us who exist are the children of successful warriors. Our history is filled with war, and those who won were permitted to procreate. They went on to make us, whereas the losers could not have their own offspring.

This observation made me think of my Catholic up-bringing and the idea of original sin. If we are all chil-dren, over the longer span of history, of those who prevailed, usually warriors or members of their camps, then all of us are guilty of violence in the past.

But should I, as a white Canadian of a certain age, living near the place where my parents created me, bear guilt for my past?

Race, privilege, guilt, and restitution are very much themes of the present moment. Exhausting themes, be-cause this notion of guilt is so all-pervasive just now. Should I feel guilty for what my people have done? And who are my people? Canadians, Lithuanians, Europeans, whites, men enamoured of toxic masculinity? Or the line of mothers who made me, or ancestors who may have been serfs bought and sold as easily as slaves, a category strangely overlooked in contemporary thinking?

I don't know the answer to this question. I think that the detour into the weighing of guilt is a step off the main path. It is one question, but not the only one.

JOSEPHINE BAKER made it all sound simple when she sang "J'ai deux amours," as if having two loves could ever be uncomplicated. But it does inoculate you from asking yourself *how* a person should be when you live intensely in parallel realities, in two different lands.

IT IS A LIFE OF SUSPENSION. Confusing sometimes, when you don't quite know which way to look. But the view is astonishing and rich for all the pain it sometimes contains, no matter which way you do choose to focus.

Anton Chekhov asks, what can we do? And he answers, we must live our lives.

In my case, both of them.

Writers and Selected Works that Have Been Mentioned in this Book

Carolyn Abraham (*The Juggler's Children*)

Edward Albee (*Who's Afraid of Virginia Woolf?*)

Svetlana Alexievich (*Voices from Chernobyl: The Oral History of a Nuclear Disaster; The Unwomanly Face of War: An Oral History of Women in World War Two*)

Andrei Amalrik (*Will the Soviet Union Survive Until 1984?*)

Martin Amis (*The Information; The War Against Cliché: Essays and Reviews 1971–2000; Koba the Dread: Laughter and the Twenty Million*)

Anne Applebaum (*Gulag: A History; Iron Curtain: The Crushing of Eastern Europe, 1944–1956*)

Margaret Atwood (*Surfacing*)

Gary Barwin (*Nothing the Same, Everything Haunted*)

Jack Belden (*Retreat with Stilwell*)

Saul Bellow (*Herzog*)

Donna Bennett and Russell Brown (*An Anthology of Canadian Literature in English*)

David Bezmozgis (*Natasha and Other Stories; Immigrant City*)

Jonas Biliūnas ("Brisiaus galas"; "Kliudžiau")

Kenneth Bonert (*The Lion Seeker*)

Andrew Borkowski (*Copernicus Avenue*)

Ray Bradbury (*The Martian Chronicles*)

Anita Brookner (*Hotel du Lac*)

Kate Brown (*A Biography of No Place: From Ethnic Borderland to Soviet Heartland*)

Cathy Marie Buchanan (*The Painted Girls*)

Jonas Budrys (*Kontražvalgyba Lietuvoje*)

John le Carré (*The Looking Glass War*)

Raymond Carver ("Cathedral")

David Chariandy (*Soucouyant*)

John Cheever (*The Stories of John Cheever*)

Wayson Choy (*The Jade Peony*)

James Clavell (*Shōgun*)

Joseph Conrad (*Nostromo; Lord Jim; The Secret Agent*)

Norman Davies (*Vanished Kingdoms: The History of Half-Forgotten Europe*)

Robertson Davies (*Fifth Business*)

Kristijonas Donelaitis ("Metai")

Leonidas Donskis (*A Small Map of Experience: Reflections and Aphorisms*)

Arthur Conan Doyle (*The Adventures of Sherlock Holmes*)

Lawrence Durrell (*The Alexandria Quartet*)

Umberto Eco (*The Book of Legendary Lands*)

Esi Edugyan (*Washington Black*)

William Faulkner (*Absalom, Absalom!*)

F. Scott Fitzgerald ("Babylon Revisited")

John Fowles (*The Magus*)

Rita Gabis (*A Guest at the Shooters' Banquet: My Grandfather's SS Past, My Jewish Family, A Search for the Truth*)

Mavis Gallant (*Paris Stories; Montreal Stories*)

Romain Gary (*La promesse de l'aube*)

Keir Giles (*Russia's War on Everybody: And What It Means For You*)

Sara Ginaite-Rubinson (*Resistance and Survival: The Jewish Community in Kaunas 1941–1944*)

Graham Greene (*The Comedians; The Quiet American*)

Algirdas Julius Greimas (*On Meaning: Selected Writings in Semiotic Theory*)

Alex Halberstadt (*Young Heroes of the Soviet Union: A Memoir and a Reckoning*)

Michael Helm (*The Projectionist*)

Ernest Hemingway (*A Farewell to Arms; The Nick Adams Stories*)

Sheila Heti (*How Should a Person Be?*)

Isabel Huggan (*Belonging: Home Away from Home*)

Tadas Ivanauskas (*Aš apsisprendžiu*)

Ted Joans (*Black Pow-Wow: Jazz Poems*)

Tony Judt (*Postwar: A History of Europe Since 1945*)

Janice Kulyk Keefer (*The Ladies' Lending Library*)

Violeta Kelertas (*Come into My Time: Lithuania in Prose Fiction, 1970–90; Marriage for Love: A Nineteenth-Century Lithuanian Woman's Fight for Justice*)

M.T. Kelly (*I Do Remember the Fall*)

Jack Kerouac (*On the Road*)

Joseph Kertes (*Winter Tulips; Gratitude; The Afterlife of Stars*)

Rudyard Kipling (*The Jungle Book*)

Petras Klimas (*Iš mano atsiminimų; Lietuvos diplomatinėje tarnyboje*)

David Knight (*Farquharson's Physique and What It Did to His Mind*)

Myrna Kostash (*Ghosts in a Photograph*)

Vincas Krėvė-Mickevičius (*Apsakymai ir padavimai*)

Rachel Kushner (*Telex from Cuba; The Flamethrowers*)

Vincent Lam (*Bloodletting & Miraculous Cures*)

Shari Lapena (*The Couple Next Door*)

Andrea Levy (*Small Island*)

Juozas Lukša, translated by Laima Vincė (*Forest Brothers: The Account of an Anti-Soviet Lithuanian Freedom Fighter, 1944–1948*)

Alistair MacLeod (*As Birds Bring Forth the Sun and Other Stories*)

Alberto Manguel (*The Library at Night*)

Justinas Marcinkevičius ("Grybų karas")

Georges Matoré (*La muselière*)

John Bentley Mays (*The Occidental Hotel*)

Jonas Mekas (*I Had Nowhere to Go*)

Icchokas Meras (*Striptizas, arba Paryžius–Roma–Paryžius*)

Adam Mickiewicz (*Pan Tadeusz*)

Jacob Mikanowski (*Goodbye Eastern Europe: An Intimate History of a Divided Land*)

Czesław Miłosz (*Native Realm: A Search for Self-Definition; The Issa Valley; The Captive Mind*)

David Mitchell (*Cloud Atlas; Black Swan Green*)

Kim Moritsugu (*The Showrunner*)

Alice Munro (*Who Do You Think You Are?*)

Henri Murger (*Scènes de la vie de bohème*)

Norman Naimark (*Stalin's Genocides*)

Edith Nesbit (*The Story of the Treasure Seekers*)

Tim O'Brien (*The Things They Carried*)

Sofi Oksanen (*When the Doves Disappeared*)

Serhii Plokhy (*The Gates of Europe: A History of Ukraine*)

Rudolf Erich Raspe (*The Surprising Adventures of Baron Munchausen*)

Nino Ricci (*Lives of the Saints; Sleep*)

Petras Rimša (*Petras Rimša pasakoja*)

Edmond Rostand (*Cyrano de Bergerac*)

Salman Rushdie (*Imaginary Homelands: Essays and Criticism 1981–1991*)

Richard Scrimger (*The Nose from Jupiter*)

Marci Shore (*The Ukrainian Night: An Intimate History of Revolution*)

Rimvydas Šilbajoris (*Perfection of Exile: Fourteen Contemporary Lithuanian Writers*)

Aušra Marija Sluckaitė-Jurašienė (*Egziliantės užrašai; Už posūkio — kitas dangus*)

Timothy Snyder (*Bloodlands: Europe Between Hitler and Stalin;*

Black Earth: The Holocaust as History and Warning)

Eva Stachniak (*The Chosen Maiden; The School of Mirrors*)

Gertrude Stein (*The Making of Americans: Being a History of a Family's Progress*)

Aleksandras Štromas (*Totalitarianism and the Prospects for World Order: Closing the Door on the Twentieth Century*)

Julija Šukys (*Siberian Exile: Blood, War, and a Granddaughter's Reckoning*)

Kenneth R. Timmerman (*The Wren Hunt; And the Rest is History: Tales of Hostages, Arms Dealers, Dirty Tricks, and Spies*)

Dylan Thomas ("A Child's Christmas in Wales"; *Under Milk Wood*)

Hunter S. Thompson (*Fear and Loathing in Las Vegas: A Savage Journey to the Heart of the American Dream*)

Kim Thúy (*Ru*)

Olga Tokarczuk (*Flights*)

John Updike (*The Collected Stories*)

H.G. Wells (*The Time Machine*)

Guy Vanderhaeghe (*The Englishman's Boy*)

Walt Whitman ("Song of Myself")

Johann David Wyss (*The Swiss Family Robinson*)

Alissa York (*Effigy; Far Cry*)

Konstantinas Žukas (*Žvilgsnis į praeitį*)

Acknowledgments

With deep thanks to George Galt, who suggested I write this book, and then made sure I did it; to eagle-eyed Snaige, who doesn't miss a thing; and to Ned Seager, who combed through so thoroughly as well.

About the Author

ANTANAS SILEIKA IS THE AUTHOR OF SIX WORKS OF fiction, including most recently the novel *Some Unfinished Business*. His short story collection *Buying on Time* was nominated for the City of Toronto Book Award and the Stephen Leacock Medal for Humour, and his novel *Provisionally Yours* has been adapted for both film and television. Beyond writing fiction, Sileika worked as a journalist and taught for many years at Humber College, eventually becoming director of the Humber School for Writers. He is now retired and lives in Toronto.